ADIRONDACK CAMP LIFE

Reflections of a Lifelong Camper

D1598769

STEVEN ROTHER

Fulton Books, Inc.
Meadville, PA

Published by Fulton Books 2020

The photo on the cover is the author's camp structure, Sunrise Cottage, constructed as a part of Camp Undercliff on Lake Placid circa 1880. Other early photos of Camp Undercliff are accessible on the Museum on Blue Mountain Lake website.

Descriptive sketches introducing each short story were drawn by Lyman Dally. Lymandally.com.

ISBN 978-1-64654-843-9 (paperback)
ISBN 978-1-64654-844-6 (digital)

Printed in the United States of America

Contents

Preface

Human identity evolves throughout early life and becomes a complex mixture of values and life goals. As we mature, we are exposed to a variety of experiences affecting our identity: religion, family customs, formal education, and personal friendships, to name just a few. Such exposure affects the labels we acquire—such as mine, *husband, father, attorney, Democrat.* But it is the much earlier life experiences that form many of the most deeply rooted values and life goals and that make each of us a unique individual.

I have given much thought to my identity and have come to the conclusion that much, if not most of it, was formed during my youthful summerlong exposures in the Adirondacks. Such exposures began in North Hudson in 1948 and have continued now through my eightieth birthday. It was those early exposures that influenced and affected me; in later life they provided enjoyment.

A goodly portion of the exposures of which I am speaking resulted from my relationships with native Adirondackers. Even today, native residents in remote sections of the Adirondacks are extraordinarily self-sufficient and quite skilled in a variety of building trades, and mechanical maintenance and repairs. In the late 1940s, well before interstate highways opened access to the Adirondacks, such independence and self-sufficiency was far more prevalent. It was my relationship with such residents, coupled with a mom who insisted that brother Davy and I pursue projects around our primitive camp, that has formed me. Even today, among other things, I still make camp plumbing repairs, and I am the only attorney I know of that owns and uses an engine hoist.

It was Dad's love of the High Peaks and nature that further influenced me. Dad would constantly take us on hikes, and along the way teach us to identify flora, fauna, and birds. Those experiences have made me very sensitive to the protection of the environment, long before concerns of global warming emerged. More significantly, my love of nature has provided me with an emotionally satisfying alternative to some formal form of religion. Now when I return to the High Peaks region, a peaceful feeling emerges.

Finally, there are many more experiences that have influenced me, which resulted from my parents' approach to childcare and summer life in the Adirondacks. From an early age, both of my parents made few attempts to control decisions made by my brother and me. Both of us were left to explore and enjoy ourselves with very little supervision. As a consequence, from a very early age we independently hiked to and camped overnight at remote ponds to fish. Doing so we encountered a variety of experiences no urban kid could ever imagine. As a result, we both matured as highly independent individuals, ready to take on the world.

I have to thank Dad for introducing me to life in the Adirondacks. Both Mom and Dad immigrated to the United States; Dad first from Germany, Mom later from Switzerland. Throughout our childhood, Mom would sit with us, flipping through the family photo albums, describing and recollecting the occasions captured. The vast majority of such photos were of Dad's and later Dad and Mom's early ventures into the High Peaks region. One of the images she frequently focused upon showed Mom and Dad standing in a meadow with a tent in the background. She would tell us that it was during their honeymoon when they camped on a meadow along the Ausable River facing Beede Farm—something she would remind us of every time we drove passed the spot.

On occasion, Dad would join us flipping through those albums. His recollections and descriptions further disclosed our family's Adirondack history. The photos showed three of Dad's early vehicles, all of them convertible roadsters with rumble seats. When Davy and I would marvel over those vehicles, he would remind us that his first trip to the Adirondacks was made hitchhiking. Frequently he would also remind us how difficult it was to reach High Peak trailheads during that time. Route 73 passing Chapel Pond had yet to be constructed, the road leading to Keene Valley and St. Hubert's being a dead end. While the roadsters looked good to me and Davy, Dad recollected how they always overheated when he traveled to Heart Lake over Cascade Pass.

I never knew the dates on which the photos were taken. However, I recently retrieved those albums and as I did so the pages began to disintegrate, leaving the photos to fall on my lap. As I collected the photos, I noticed that on the rear of each Dad had written a date, and on some even a description of the scene. Even better, among the photos were a number of postcards. From the messages on those cards, I learned the dates when Dad first climbed White Face and Marcy.

To my surprise, I learned that Dad made his first trip to the Adirondacks in 1929, within a year of his migration to this country. From the photos, it appears that Dad came to the High Peaks every year thereafter, stopping only when World War II began. He returned in 1947, brought the family to Sharp Bridge campsite in 1948 and purchased our North Hudson camp in 1949. Obviously, the gap in his pilgrimages to the High Peaks was caused by World War II gas rationing. Dad didn't serve in that war as he worked for RCA, where he had been involved in design and production of radar from its inception.

The purchase of our camp in 1949 was the best thing Dad could have done for his family. He purchased that camp a decade before he purchased our first family home on the New Jersey shore. At the time he made the purchase, he did so hoping he could find employment in or near the North Country; to his disappointment, he never did. But for that first year Davy and I attended Schroon Lake Central School, and we lived in that rustic camp with no central heat, no electricity, and no running water. That may sound like a primitive lifestyle, but for Davy and me it positively added to our formative life experiences.

What's a Camp?

I get a variety of responses when I tell people in New Jersey that "I am going to my camp." Some respond with a quizzical expression, and occasionally they ask, "You own a children's camp?" But most often the response is a simple "What's a camp?" My usual response is a paraphrasing of a description I once read in a history of the Adirondacks—it goes something like this: it all started in the nineteenth century when early guides built crude shelters in the woods for clients in pursuit of fish and game, which they quite logically called camps. Those shelters evolved into more durable lean-tos or tents on platforms. Slowly the term morphed into a description of a seasonal structure that can be anything from a rustic one-room cabin to more elaborate structures in the woods.

In recent years, I have given more thought to the use of the word *camp*, and I have concluded that some folks have taken great liberty with that term, liberties with which Seneca Ray Stoddard, or even Marjorie Merriweather Post would have difficulty. Having been an eighty-plus-year observer of the evolution of Adirondack camp life, I have here exercised a point of privilege to more precisely define the term and to make clear to my readers what constitutes a camp and, more importantly, what does not. However, before doing so, and in the process offending many newcomers to the Adirondacks, I should describe my introduction camp life as a youth and how that has affected my definition of *camp*.

Nearly all of my childhood summers were spent at my parents' camp in North Hudson. That four-room structure was located several miles up a then-unnamed dirt road, without electric service or running water. For some years we cooked on a woodstove, lighted the night with kerosene lamps, relieved ourselves in an outhouse, and kept perishables in an icebox—yes, a real icebox with a compartment for a block of ice, which drained into a pan requiring frequent emptying. Without doubt this structure qualified as a camp, but I am getting ahead of myself.

Dad, an electrical engineer, joined us at camp on weekends and for his annual two-week vacation. An inveterate hiker, Dad wanted nothing to do but climb mountains during his limited time in the Adirondacks. Only after much prodding from Mom would he ever undertake chores around the camp. During the week Mom would put Brother Davy and me to work fetching water from a spring, splitting wood and other chores. As we grew older, we were put to work painting the camp, a chore which never seemed to end.

Over time, as the camp first was electrified and then later connected to the spring, Dad engaged Norman Clark to make these improvements and repairs, the need for which were discovered each spring as camp was reopened. Norm, as we called him, was typical of the North Country natives I have met; he held several jobs and was quite skilled in many trades. During the school year Norm drove a school bus for the Schroon Lake Central School, and while classes were in session, he performed maintenance and repairs on the school bus fleet. During the summer recess and on weekends, he was engaged by camp owners, like Dad, to make repairs and improvements.

Norm frequently brought his son Gary with him when he worked on our camp. Gary was my age and served as Norm's assistant and all-around craftsman in training. I tagged along, at first just as an observer, but soon competed with Gary to help Norm in any way possible. Norm took frequent cigarette breaks and while taking long drags on unfiltered Chesterfields would explain why he used a particular tool or what he would do next. In the process I learned some of the basics of carpentry and electrical and plumbing work. In retrospect I have come to understand this process as a North Country rite of passage. In a place and time where self-sufficiency and the ability to earn a living by many means was essential, these skills were the measure of North Country survival.

Each summer I would acquire basic tools that I would add to my collection. While Norm continued to perform more extensive work, I began to look for and make simple repairs. Then during the summer of my fifteenth year, I was offered a job to assist in the construction of a new camp a short distance down our road. For the next two summers I was exposed to every aspect of construction, from the pouring of a foundation to the backbreaking work of laying roofing shingles. By the time the camp was completed, I had attained a fair level of proficiency in a number of trades. From these experiences, I have taken a lifelong profound respect for those who work with their hands, but even more, I have come to admire the self-sufficiency that comes with the acquisition of such skills.

And so it was when I turned twenty-seven and was offered the opportunity to purchase, on very reasonable terms, a broken-down camp on Lake Placid, I eagerly accepted. The dilapidated condition of the structure was not viewed as a burden, but rather a challenge to my now well-developed pioneering sense of self-sufficiency. The fact that the camp was only accessible by water simply enhanced that feeling.

It is with this background that I have come to the task of defining the word *camp*. In so doing, I understand that times have changed, as have the expectations of part-time residents of the Adirondacks. The Interstate Highway System now enables families from Boston, New York, and even more distant places easy access to all of the park, without the inconveniences experienced by my parents. Moreover, with the passage of time, the expectations for creature comforts have increased. But we cannot let these developments erode the concept of *camp*, lest the term become synonymous with *house*. As true camps can take many forms, rather than attempt a definition of camp, I have decided to list those attributes that render a structure and place ineligible for that coveted appellation. Those disqualifications are few, but very telling.

A camp is a structure for periodic and seasonal use, winter use being brief and with some attendant discomfort. Therefore, if your place in the Adirondacks has central heat and a plumbing system that functions 365 days a year, you don't have a camp, you have a house in the woods.

Camp is a term that describes more than structure, it describes place. Therefore, if your place abuts a road that includes the words *route, highway, avenue,* or similar term, you don't have a camp. In fact, if you can hear road noise or FedEx can find you, you don't have a camp.

I was going to disqualify those who have granite countertops in their kitchens, but gave up the notion lest I become too critical. However, if your place has a swimming pool or an exercise room, forget about calling it a camp.

Finally, if your place has a lawn and well-manicured landscaping, as Norm would say, "That ain't no camp!" Worse yet, if you fertilize that lawn and douse it with pesticides, leave now, go home, and never cross the Blue Line again.

Route 9 Gypsies

Whenever a new acquaintance first learns that I have a camp on Lake Placid, I am invariably asked the same two questions. How long is the drive? How often do you make the trip? When told that my family and I make the six-hundred-mile round trip from New Jersey nearly every weekend, ice-out through mid-October, most react as though I am not in possession of all my faculties. It is not as though I become an object of derision, the response is usually limited to one of those sideways looks or a stare over lowered eyeglasses, the kind of look that clearly expresses a measure of disbelief. Realizing that by most standards my weekly trek is extraordinary, I feel compelled to defend myself. Of course, I could do this by extolling the beauty of the Adirondacks or the peacefulness of our secluded camp. Though usually, I take a different tack—one best described as "comparative sanity."

"That's nothing," I begin. "When I was a kid, before the Thruway, my dad would drive eight to ten hours up old Route 9 to his camp in North Hudson."

At this point in the conversation the listener's look quickly changes. The realization sets in that he has been trapped into listening to some lengthy monologue, one usually delivered by an elder citizen about long hikes through snowdrifts to get to school. Most times a hastily contrived excuse for leaving aborts the telling of earlier family migrations. Occasionally the skeptic lacks the ability to fashion an excuse, and I proceed.

My first trip to the Adirondacks occurred in 1948, a two-week stay at Sharp Bridge state campsite in North Hudson. It was a year later that my parents purchased a camp in North Hudson. Dad had been coming to the Adirondacks since 1929, drawn to Keene Valley by the High Peaks. At first he came as a hitchhiker, but soon he commenced our family's auto marathon which was only interrupted by the gas rationing of World War II.

Before 1949 our sojourns in the Adirondacks were sporadic, but with the purchase of the camp things changed. During summer school vacation Mom Davy and I would stay at camp, Dad joining us during his vacation and on weekends. During spring and fall we began to make weekly weekend pilgrimages. I say this as for Dad these trips were in a very real sense a pilgrimage. As near as I could determine, the time he spent climbing mountains constituted a religious experience. Furthermore, the difficulties encountered at that time in traveling from New Jersey to North Hudson rivaled a journey to Mecca. Routes 17, 9W and 9, as they wound their way through every city and hamlet were the most direct route. We would pass through scores of places like Sloatsburg and Cementon, each punctuated with numerous traffic lights. In addition, in most places the highway had but one lane in either direction. The ever present truck traffic would severely impede progress.

To Dad these were minor inconveniences one had to endure in order to enjoy Adirondack vistas from above the tree line. After all, he had suffered the uncertainties inherent in hitchhiking. Mom, on the other hand, was the caregiver of two children and found the trips an ordeal.

Intent on devising a regimen to ease Mom's burden, Dad altered our departure schedule and made some major revisions to the family car. Dad decided that commencing our journey at the close of business on Friday afternoons was not desirable. Even if he left work an hour or so early, we could still expect to encounter heavy local traffic at least through Albany. He therefore decided that he and Mom would nap until 10:00 or 10:30 p.m. Five hours of sleep would leave them refreshed for a drive that would meet with far less traffic. Furthermore, there would be the added bonus of traffic lights that at that late hour became amber flashes.

According to Dad's plan, my brother Davy and I would make the trip, Pullman-style, in the back of the Chevy. Dad had removed the rear seat and installed a piece of plywood, which ran from the front seat into the trunk. Over the plywood he placed a mattress. Dad planned to bed us down right after supper, while the car was parked in the garage. Mom would of course have nothing to do with that part of his plan. When Dad's scheme finally went into operation we went to sleep in our beds and, at the time of departure, were carried to the car, wrapped in blankets.

At this point, Dad's plan hit a major snag. Our car, a 1937 Chevy, had a clipped trunk. With my head near the front seat, my feet nearly reached the trunk lid. There was precious little space left for the gear we invariably had in tow, not to mention the steady stream of hand-me-downs provided by friends and family to furnish the camp. Most importantly, there was no room for the numerous spare tires we would require. I am not sure whether Goodyear was still in the dark ages or all the good tires had been bolted to military vehicles. In any event, I have a vivid recollection of Dad making at least one, and sometimes two, tire changes during each leg of the trip. Dad would have loved to purchase another vehicle, perhaps a new station wagon. However, this near to the end of the war new cars were very scarce. Hence, he began to explore alternatives. An engineer by training, Dad was up to the challenge.

The first option was a roof rack. Not finding a commercially made rack to his liking, Dad began designing his own on an old drafting table in the basement. After several evenings' work, he called Mom to the basement for a consultation. I can still hear her plaintive tones as she said, "You mean to put all those tires on the roof? We'll look like Okies!"

Dad didn't go back to the drawing board. The next solution came from the pages of *Popular Mechanics*. For that reason, Mom took this suggestion very seriously—he proposed to build a trailer. Dad assured Mom that the trailer would look very smart. He showed her the photos in the magazine. There was the author, arms akimbo, with one foot braced on the tire of his prototype. Dad even promised to paint the trailer to match the Chevy. Mom, always sensitive to appearances, wasn't quite certain. "We won't look like a bunch of gypsies?" she asked. Dad assured her that trailers were the new rage, and soon everyone would be towing one.

The article was very thorough. It provided Dad with a parts list, required tools, and helpful hints how to scrounge parts and materials from junkyards. In the garage he began to assemble a sizable pile of angle iron, axles, bearings, springs, hubs, rims, and tires. Dad was proud of the fact that with the exception of a hitch purchased at Pep Boys, all parts had been acquired in junkyards. Mom watched the greasy pile grow with ever-increasing anxiety.

When at last he had gathered all the necessary components, Dad confided in Mom that he lacked an essential tool to complete the job. He would need to cut and weld heavy gage metal—an acetylene torch was required. After some deliberation, Dad decided to solve the problem at the RCA plant in Harrison, New Jersey, his place of employment.

The euphemism "defense work" was in frequent use during those times. It conjured up images of defense plant workers carting goodies home in briefcases and lunch pails. For Dad the process worked in reverse. Each day he would take another grimy part with him to the plant. In a quiet corner, he and a befriended welder began to cut and fuse the pieces together.

Bringing material into the plant did not pose much of a problem; the guards had been trained to look for movements in the opposite direction. Bringing the completed trailer out was another story. A log was maintained at the guardhouse, wherein was maintained a record of the comings and goings of all vehicles. No one had made an entry of the arrival of this strange little two-wheeled vehicle, and why was this guy (Dad) trying to pull it through the gate. We kids were never told the details, but I can remember fits of hysterical laughter whenever Dad's coworkers came to our home and recalled the event.

And so began our late Friday-night stints, trailer in tow, Davy and I cutting Zs in the back. Although not perfect, Dad's new regimen was much improved over the earlier departure. However, Mom's esthetic concerns were not assuaged. Each trip she would declare that we looked like gypsies. Such pronouncements came more frequently should the trailer be loaded high with hand-me-downs. But Mom also found the new schedule an improvement, and so found a way to tolerate Dad's love affair with the mountains.

Sleeping in the back of the Chevy was good training for the business travel I would suffer in later life. Over time business associates marvel at how readily I could fall asleep on a plane or train. Although comfortable enough, Davy and I were surrounded by a cacophony of sound. On the trip north, Dad would drone on about the camp, the hike he planned, the hike he had made the previous week. Besides the normal road noise there was a metal-against-metal clanking sound—a sound that took on a rhythmic cadence as the trailer bumped over seams in the road. In our younger years we would frequently ask what that sound was. Dad would always respond, "It's the shackles on the trailer—lousy design—I'll fix it next week." But soon Dad's voice and the measured sound of the shackles would blend and take on a hypnotic quality. Usually we would sleep through Warrensburg or Chestertown.

With Warrensburg came morning light. Soon Davy and I would be on our knees, hanging over the front seat. Mom usually nodded out by then. Dad, eager for a new audience, would now regale us with the wonder of things inside the Blue Line. Dad cited mountain facts like a baseball fan batting statistics. He was a walking, talking trail guide. During one of Dad's oral tours he would not only recite mountain altitudes, but he also gave you his personal best time to the summit.

Although Dad would hike in the company of others, he frequently did so alone. Dressed in shorts and high topped Keds, a small army surplus bag over the shoulder, he would dash up and over as many peaks as daylight would permit. Frequently fading light would leave him miles from his destination. He would then bushwhack and hitch his way back to the Chevy. Mom would be waiting anxiously with supper grown cold.

Sundays were spent puttering about camp. Mom forbid hiking on Sunday as she insisted upon a 2:00 p.m. departure. The return trip had a different quality. For one, Dad became less talkative, more introspective. Davy and I, tuckered from a weekend in the woods, would play games in the back of the Chevy. Somewhere south of Albany sleep would overtake us, and we would morph back to the life of city folk.

With the passage of time, some things changed. In the early 1950s Dad got his new station wagon. Slowly the trip was shortened as first the Thruway was constructed in stages, and later the Northway was completed. Throughout all this the trailer, to Mom's chagrin, continued to tag along on more trips than she would have liked. Dad always had some reason, real or contrived, to take it along.

I have followed in Dad's footsteps; in 1969 I purchased the camp on Lake Placid. As Davy and I were carried to the Adirondacks every weekend, so I have carted my own children on many a weekend. I have even found myself regaling the kids with Adirondack trivia on the trip north, only to fall silent on the return trip. I think I have come to understand this apparent manic/depressive behavior. It's the anticipation that gets you there and the memories that get you back.

My vehicles have always been quite suitable for such treks, usually larger four-by-fours. However, like Dad, I have occasionally taken to hauling a trailer. (Now it was the family of my wife, Mary, that gave us the hand-me-downs.) In fact, it's not just any old trailer, it's *the* trailer, a bequest I valued and passed on to Davy's son. When the kids were younger, they used to ask me what that strange clanking noise was. I would tell them, "It's the shackles—lousy design—I'll fix it next week."

Poached Trout

S hould you have begun reading on the assumption that I have written about the preparation of fish, please stop. Do yourself a favor, reach instead for your *New York Times* or Julia Child cookbook. No, this is not a recipe, it's a confession—a long-overdue confession. This story involves that other kind of poaching: a sordid tale of premeditation, trespass, and other high crimes.

Lest you fear that I am about to embark on some legally ill-advised disclosure, rest easy. Miranda warnings are not necessary. I am a law school graduate admitted to practice law in a distant state that shall remain nameless. Furthermore, although I have not researched the matter, I feel quite confident that sufficient time has passed so that some statute of limitations will protect me from this indiscretion. And then of course there are a host of mitigating circumstances such as... But wait, in my haste to rub balm on my conscience, I have gotten ahead of myself. Let me instead give you the facts in chronological sequence and you, the reader, be the judge of any misdeeds.

It all began in the summer of 1952. Our family, as usual, was well settled for the summer at our camp in North Hudson. Mom, my brother Davy, and I were in residence for the duration while Dad joined us on weekends. Life progressed as it had in past summers. During the week Davy and I did what we liked best—trout fishing. On the weekends we joined Dad doing what he liked best—climbing the High Peaks. Dad much preferred hiking over trout fishing, but he sure did like to eat fresh trout. The whole family did.

At this point I should tell you that in 1952 I was twelve years of age and Davy was nine. We were an adventuresome pair and by that age had gotten to fish many of the streams in our half of Essex County. Mom would fix us lunch and drop us off on the Schroon, East Branch, Boquet, or other river. We would spend the day wading in our sneakers to some distant point where Mom was scheduled to retrieve us. Most days we were successful. During the early weeks of the season we rarely got skunked.

How we achieved our success was another matter. Today I have acquired a certain degree of stream etiquette. I adhere to the catch-and-release philosophy, have tied a few flies, and can present a fly with some deftness. In 1952 Davy and I were what would be disparagingly referred to today as "meat" fishermen. Artificials had little appeal to us. Grasshoppers and worms, preferably big fat night crawlers, were the bait of choice. But of course, Dad didn't fish, so our only role models were a few of the local residents, who like us were meat fishermen.

Our eagerness to fill our creels wasn't totally unbridled. Mom had emigrated from Switzerland, Dad from Germany, and both brought with them an almost slavish adherence to *the law*. Early each summer Dad would stop at the town clerk's office and secure a copy of the fish-and-game regulations. He would then instruct us as to the size and creel limits we were to observe. We were also advised of special restrictions on streams that we frequented. Over breakfast we could expect to be quizzed on these commandments of the New

York State Conservation Department. All this made our subsequent indiscretion all the more surprising.

Our tale begins to take shape later that summer; my recollection puts it in early August. Dad's sister, Tante Emma, was to visit her family in this country. It was decided that the entire clan—aunts, uncles, cousins, the whole bunch—would join us at camp for a week-long reunion. Most of the adults would sleep indoors; the kids would sleep in tents. It was gonna be great!

Davy and I looked forward to this family gathering with ever heightened anticipation. In particular, we looked forward to spend time with one particular cousin. He was considerably older than we were, but not so old that we considered him an adult. He did have a car and liked to fish trout, a combination that bode well for us—or perhaps not as you will soon learn. His name was Gunther. The cousins all called him "Gunt," with decidedly anglicized pronunciation.

The appointed day finally arrived. The weather was clear and comfortably warm. It was late in the afternoon, and the whole clan seemed to arrive at once. The camp, usually quite peaceful, became a mass of humanity. As each car arrived the occupants, after greeting each other warmly, set about emptying its contents of duffel, tents, and enormous quantities of food. The men began erecting tents while the women prepared the evening meal. The tents having been erected, Dad engaged all willing hands in the chore of constructing one of his "campfires." This activity involved dragging every piece of downed timber from the surrounding woods and creating a pile in the meadow at the front of the camp. The bigger the pile, the better.

The evening meal was one of those memorable childhood events. Each of my aunts had prepared some specialty dish. My favorite was the warm potato salad with bacon. The meal was accompanied by lots of storytelling, jokes, and general revelry. As the family had heard of Davy's and my fishing prowess, much good-natured ribbing was directed at us. We were told that our luck had better be good as there were many mouths to feed. Before long, the younger cousins picked up on the theme, and soon we were taunted by a singsongy "better catch some fiish, better catch some fiish."

When the sun finally set, Dad called everyone to his campfire and with much fanfare set it ablaze. Uncle Herman brought out his guitar and led the group in choruses of "Jimmy Cracks Corn" and "I've Been Working on the Railroad." As the flames began to die down, Dad pulled his usual stunt. He jumped over the fire—right through the flames. Mom, as always, covered her eyes and naturally all the kids wanted to follow suit. The aunts then interceded and the stunts ended for the evening as the younger cousins were hustled off to bed.

Gunt, Davy, and I stayed by the fire, a short distance from where the men continued to sit, talk, and take occasional pokes at the coals. As we lay on our stomachs, staring into the embers, our conversation quickly turned to fishing. Trout fishing of course. "Where are we going to catch enough trout to feed this crowd?" Gunt asked. Davy and I both admitted that our luck had been off during the past week. It was late in the season, it had been warm, and water levels were low. Not the conditions for successful trout fishing.

"We'll never survive this week if we don't catch fish—lots of fish," I observed.

"Where can we catch trout this time of year?" asked Gunt.

"In a few deep holes," I responded

We continued to stare into the fire. After a while Gunt stood up and gave us each a knowing look. "I've got an idea," he said. And some idea it was! We would use Gunt's car to drive as close as possible to each of the many holes Davy and I knew, thereby concentrating our efforts only on those spots where trout might be holding. If we moved fast, we might be able to cover all the holes we knew on the Boreas, Schroon, East Branch, and Boquet, not to mention some of their tributaries. With this plan whirling in our heads, we retried to get an early start the following morning.

First light found us very quietly making preparations. We knew that should any of the cousins wake they would want to come, and we would be forced to take them. Some cold cereal was quickly wolfed down, and our gear was loaded into Gunt's car. While I packed lunch Davy, with little success, tried to catch some grasshoppers in the meadow. The dew was still quite heavy, and the hoppers hadn't yet become active. We jumped in Gunt's car and drove down our lane toward Route 9.

At the bottom of the lane, near its intersection with Route 9, was Dewey Duntley's farm. Old Dewey kept a few Holsteins and had accumulated a sizable manure pile behind his cowshed. Some years before, Dewey had invited us to dig worms in that pile, an invitation we acted upon with regularity. Although Dewey was far too old and unsteady to wade trout streams, he had been a meat fisherman in his time and had passed along more than a few fishing tips to Davy and me.

With just a few turns of a shovel, we were able to collect enough modest-sized fishing worms to satisfy our needs. With a pat on the head for Dewey's dog, we were off and running. Leaving the Duntley farm, we turned South on Route 9 and headed for Blue Ridge. We planned to drive up Blue Ridge Road to the Boreas River and then work our way back up Route 9 to Route 78, ending our trip in Keene Valley. Along the way we would be able to park within reasonable walking distance of holes on many of our regular rivers and streams. Gunt's car, a Nash Rambler, was perfect for this exercise. It was a wagon-like vehicle in which we could quickly stow our fly rods without the need for breaking them down.

By noon it became apparent that despite all our planning the dinner table would be troutless that evening. Nonetheless we continued and by late afternoon had reached Keene Valley without a single keeper in our creel. We had just come down the steep grade from Chapel Pond and parked where the East Branch approaches from the west and crosses under the road. On the west side of the road, at the base of a steep cliff, is a very large hole. We made our way down an embankment at the bridge and over a rocky bar to the edge of the pool.

The pool was large enough so that all three of us could comfortably take positions along its edge. Gunt was at the head of the pool fishing a small fly weighted with shot and dressed with a half-inch of worm. He said it was for "taste." Davy and I were using snelled Eagle Claws, threaded lengthwise through the worm so that the hook was completely covered and then stitched several times through the

23

loose end. The sun had passed behind the trees, and only a few rays shone through the branches. The water was quite cold, but my feet had become numb some hours earlier. It had been at Sharp Bridge that I was last conscious of the small stones and other debris in my sneakers.

Each of us allowed the slow-moving current to take our bait for several passes along the cliff's edge. Now you could see the bait as the current gently boiled to the surface, then it would disappear into the depths of the pool. It was on the third or fourth pass that Gunt got a strike. It was a small brookie, just barely a keeper. He unhooked it and tossed it on the bank. We continued to fish in silence, the brookie flopping about on the river stone behind us. The sunlight continued to fade, and we knew that we were in for a ration of ribbing.

Gunt was the first to get zapped by a mosquito and announced that it was time to get back to camp and face the music. As Davy and I broke down our rods, Gunt cleaned his trout at the water's edge. As he squatted there in the half-light he said, "You know, maybe we should've started here today. Maybe we should start here tomorrow and fish upstream."

"Can't," I said.

"Why not," he asked.

"Cause there's a private preserve up there," I replied in as serious a tone as I could muster, while pointing upstream.

We made our way back to the Nash and stowed our gear. After a brief argument as to who would ride shotgun, we headed South on 73. We had not reached Chapel Pond when Gunt began to quiz us about the preserve. Davy and I explained that many of our hikes with Dad began with a walk through the preserve, a large area owned by a private club. We told him of the long dirt road that was closed to cars and which provided access to trailheads. We told him of the mother of all fishing holes, a small man-made impoundment along that road and the huge breeder trout that lay about in it. Gunt was incredulous.

"How big do you say these fish are?"

Davy and I crossed arms in the front seat as we each tried to demonstrate. During the balance of the return trip we were completely absorbed in a conversation about the size and number of trout in that impoundment.

When we got back to camp, dinner was just about over. We were greeted by Dad, Uncle Herman, and an assortment of cousins. The first words out of their mouths was "How many fish did you catch?" Reluctantly we admitted failure—one fish caught. The cousins all wanted to see the fish, a request we were obviously not eager to obey. By now others had gathered about, all exhorting us to show the fish. The pressure was too great; the brookie was produced. Hoots and hollers followed. Dad ventured that it wasn't legal. Davy tugged at the jaw and tail to demonstrate its full length, while Gunt mumbled something about how fish shrivel once out of water.

The three of us beat a hasty retreat to the kitchen where we served ourselves from the plentiful leftovers. We then sat at a picnic table behind the camp so as to avoid further embarrassing encounters—to no avail. We were soon found by many and subjected to further humiliation. Uncle Herman, strumming the tune "Ain't Gonna Make War No More" on his guitar, ad-libbed lyrics about not catching trout.

Purely as a defensive move we retired early that night. Davy and I had invited Gunt to bunk with us. We slept in a tent erected on a permanent platform in a stand of pines behind the camp. Although we retired early, we didn't fall asleep for hours. The conversation, mostly about fishing, took many turns. One topic we returned to again and again was those breeders in the preserve. I can't recollect today who it was that first suggested it, but sometime well after midnight we agreed to become poachers.

Everyone was up and about quite early the following morning. While we retired early the previous evening, plans had been made for this day. One group was to be led by Dad on an expedition up Giant Mountain. A second group was to go with Uncle Herman for a speedboat ride on Lake Placid. As we had not planned the details of our caper, we ate our breakfast slowly, waiting for camp to clear out. Time and again we were asked to join one or the other group. Each time we declined saying that we wished to try our luck once more.

Once the last car finally disappeared down the lane, we began to scheme. Davy and I had to dissuade Gunt of the idea of carrying rods into the preserve. We would have to walk a long distance up the dirt road, and there was no way to conceal rods, even if disassembled. Gunt deferred to us and suggested drop lines or saplings to be cut on location. And so each of us prepared a ten-foot length of monofilament line affixed to a hook and some shot.

This day we would have many grasshoppers. The sun was already quite high, and Davy and I quickly filled a Skippy peanut butter jar with several dozen hoppers. That jar, the drop lines, a container of worms we would dig from Dewey's manure pile, and our lunch would be carried in a knapsack. In lieu of a creel, Gunt would wear his field jacket, which had a large game pocket in the back. We would look like ordinary hikers on a day trip.

It was about 10:00 a.m. when we finally headed north in the Nash. We parked at the Noonmark trailhead and began to walk. The first several hundred yards were in the open, along a golf course and some tennis courts. As the day was very warm, Gunt shed his field jacket and slung it over his shoulder. Soon we came to a gate with the club's initials formed rustic style at the center. Conspicuously posted at the spot provided for pedestrian access was a sign. Years earlier Dad had read us the sign: rules, regulations, admonitions about fishing. That day we hurried on.

We were now walking under very large deciduous trees. The air was much cooler, and filled with the aroma of duff and damp leaves. We walked abreast at a brisk pace without talking. After about fifteen minutes we encountered an elderly man walking in the opposite direction. He greeted us and praised the weather. In passing he looked me square in the eye, and for the first time that day I felt fear. Could he perhaps tell what we were up to? Mom always claimed she could see mischief in our eyes. I said nothing, and we continued on our way.

Further along we heard the distant sound of running water. Davy and I knew we would shortly come upon the stream that flowed from the impoundment. It's a beautiful little stream that cuts between moss-covered boulders and falls into shimmering, crystal-clear pools.

As we walked along its banks, I could feel my heartbeat increase. The road made several turns, crested a modest grade, and there it was.

The impoundment was formed by an eight-foot-high stone and concrete dam across the stream. Behind the dam was a body of water perhaps 500 feet square. The road passed very close to the pool, less than ten feet. A low stone wall had been erected along the water's edge along the road. On the far side of the pool was a large rock ledge that dropped some three feet to the surface of the water. The inlet to the pool came over several large boulders and ledges. The sound of flowing water, both incoming and outgoing, created a fair din.

We approached the wall and peered into the crystal-clear water. The shallowest portion of the pool was at the base of the wall. The deepest portion was on the far side, along the rock ledge where the current created ripples and small waves. Despite the surface disturbance, fish were clearly visible. There were at least a dozen along the far edge, all facing upstream, maintaining their position with just the slightest tail movement. My heartbeat kicked up another notch. In unison we made furtive glances over our shoulders. Gunt suggested in a whispered tone that we should move to the far ledge.

We quickly made our way across the stream below the dam and crept to the edge of the ledge on all fours. From this vantage point, we were looking nearly straight down, and it was apparent how large these trout were. These were hefty fish, each displaying the telltale white outline of a brook trout on their fins. We lay motionless for a while watching as they held their positions in the current. Now and again one would move a short distance for some morsel and then return to its post. Gunt spoke first in a tone just loud enough to be heard over the sound of the running water: "Let's cut some switches."

We backed away from the ledge on all fours, stood up, and retreated some distance into the woods. Well out of sight of passersby, we each set about cutting a sapling from a stand of immature beaches. As we were stripping the small branches with our pocketknives, I asked, "How are we going to do this? Someone might walk by."

"We'll sit on the ledge with our lunches. If someone comes, we'll ditch the poles and make like we're taking a break," Gunt said.

Before returning to the ledge, we each attached our lines to the poles and baited up with worms. We decided on worms as hoppers were more buoyant and would be difficult to float to the depths at which these trout were holding. Poles in hand, we returned to the ledge in a crouched walk. Gunt took a position nearest the dam while I took the head of the pool, Davy between us. We conspicuously displayed the knapsack on the ledge and unwrapped our sandwiches. Why Davy and I had removed the Skippy jar is still a mystery. In any event it was set on the ledge between us.

I was the first one to get my bait into the water. I made a little underhand cast and let the current take the worm down toward the trout. My state of consciousness was in some disarray. I could now feel my heart beating in my throat, and although aware that Davy and Gunt were speaking to each other, I could not discern what they said. I do remember thinking that the fish must have seen us and be sufficiently spooked not to strike.

As my bait approached the lead fish, it swam forward and inhaled. I could now hear Gunt's excited voice, "You got one! You got one!" The fish dropped back to its lead position, and I sat there in shock. It now became clear to me that the largest trout—no, the largest fish of any kind that I had ever caught—was at the other end of a very primitive rig. How was I going to land this monster? How was I going to get this monster up and over the ledge?

I continued to sit there watching the fish, to which I had become connected. I was sure that it had swallowed the bait as it began to show signs of some discomfort—little sideways movements. The current must have started to exert pressure on the line and in turn on the hook. I got into a crouched position and gave the pole a short, but very firm, jolt to be sure the hook was set.

From this point on, the sequence of events are not completely clear to me. I can remember the trout heading upstream while I tried to follow, all the while attempting to keep the line from tangling in the branches of overhanging trees. The fish finally came to rest in the depths at the base of the ledge. There on my hands and knees, I took hold of the line and hauled the fish, hand over hand, out of the water and over the ledge. The last few knuckle-bloodying seconds were spent trying to subdue the fish as it flipped about on the stone.

I had no sooner gotten my thumb and index finger under the gill covers when Gunt said, "Ditch the fish, someone's coming." Behind the ledge was a fair-sized depression created when a large tree had blown down. As I turned to toss the fish into the depression, I kicked the Skippy jar. It clinked and clattered down the ledge and came to rest in the water, twist cap up. Gunt moaned.

A middle-aged couple appeared at the wall and immediately engaged us in conversation. It took a few moments for me to regain my composure. As I did, I took stock of our situation and concluded that we were in deep trouble. The Skippy jar was now bobbing in the water near the dam while the surface of the water beneath the ledge was covered with bits of moss and twigs, the debris from my battle with the fish. Both Gunt and Davy had stowed their poles in the brush behind them, but I could see that they had left bait and lines in the water. As they munched on their sandwiches, Gunt and Davy conversed with the couple. I could hear the trout thrashing about in the leaves behind me.

The couple volunteered that they had just returned from a guide-boat trip to Upper Ausable Lake, a surefire sign that they were club members. They asked where we were headed, and Davy responded that as we had gotten a late start, we were only going to climb Indian Head, a low stone outcropping at the end of the road. The conversation then turned to the recent blowdowns and the condition of trails. I managed to make some observation as to the state of the trail through Hunter's Pass, something I had heard from Dad. Slowly the couple bid us farewell. None too soon as out of the corner of my eye I observed a fish take Gunt's bait.

As the couple disappeared down the road, I leapt for my fish and began the chore of removing the hook. The trout had indeed swallowed the hook, and I was having a devilish time retrieving it. As I struggled there in the depression, I could hear the hushed whispers of Gunt and Davy. They were catching fish while I was stuck in the innards of my first fish. In desperation I pulled hard on the line until I drew the fish's gut through its mouth. I cut the hook free with my knife and returned to the ledge in search of bait. Davy was in the midst of landing a fish as I searched through the knapsack for the worms.

"Forget it, we're leaving," Gunt said.

"But I only caught one fish," I protested.

"Wanna get caught, keep fishin," Gunt responded.

As Davy wrestled with his fish, Gunt took the knapsack from me and into it stuffed the remainder of lunch. He then slid my fish into the game pocket of his jacket. It quickly became clear to me that if I still had the stomach for fishing, I would be doing it alone. Davy handed Gunt his fish, which also disappeared into the game pocket, and we were off. As we passed under the dam, Gunt stepped up on a larger boulder and snagged the Skippy jar.

Gunt took the lead and set a brisk pace. Davy and I with much shorter legs had to break into occasional trots in order to keep up. As I followed I noted a heavy sag in Gunt's jacket and asked how many fish we caught. I was advised that Gunt and Davy had each caught two for a total of five. By the time we reached the gate, blood was oozing through Gunt's jacket, no doubt from the mauling I had given my trout. Gunt carried the jacket folded on itself and over his shoulder for the rest of the walk.

With a sigh of relief and no arguments about riding shotgun, we jumped into the Nash. As we passed the Giant trailhead, I observed Dad's car. It was only 2:30 p.m., and the hikers wouldn't be back at camp for several hours.

We made several stops on the way back. The first was along the Bouquet River so that we could clean our catch. In all the excitement back at the impoundment, we did not have the opportunity to examine our trophies. Gunt and Davy engaged in a brief wrangling over who caught which fish. Given its disfigurement, there was absolutely no doubt which one was mine. And lucky for me that is was so identifiable. My catch was far and away the largest of the five. It was quite obviously a male, which had developed a pronounced hook to its jaw. I felt better now even though I only caught one fish.

The second stop was a little roadside refreshment stand that years ago stood at the intersection of Routes 73 and 9. For many years, the Perkins family ran the stand during the summer months, returning to Florida for the rest of the year. Dad had made a tradition of stopping there for ice cream after a hike. Gunt treated and as always Mr. Perkins quizzed us about our fishing luck. We did admit to having fished, but told him we had quit early after catching only five small trout. Mr. Perkins was far too experienced a fisherman to risk showing him our catch.

On reaching camp we wrapped our catch, stowed it in the fridge, and sat back to await the return of the family. Mom, Dad, and the Giant hikers were the first to return. It was instantly clear that they too had stopped at the refreshment stand. As they rolled out of the car, some of the cousins made comments about small trout and Dad advised us that Mr. Perkins had spilled the beans about our poor fishing fortunes.

In a repeat of the previous night's ritual everyone gathered in the kitchen to observe the catch. Mom fumbled about in the fridge looking for the fish. "They must be here somewhere. They can't be *that* small," she said to everyone's glee. And then after several moments more of searching about she finally withdrew holding a huge package. "Oh my! Oh my!" she kept repeating as she laid the package on the kitchen table. Just as she began to unwrap the package, Uncle Herman and the Lake Placid travelers returned. The whole family now crowded about as the contents were revealed.

Exclamations of every type were uttered. Mom expressed the belief that these were not trout, as she had never seen trout half the size. One of the uncles was heard asking Dad how far it was to the nearest fish market. Lucky for us, in those days there were none. But it was Uncle Herman who made a positive identification. He told everyone that he had observed a man catch trout this size, some even with hooked jaws, from the Madison River in Wyoming. Uncle Herman generally considered a reliable source, our bona fides were no longer open to question. And so it was that the catch was photographed, made into fillets, cooked, and eaten. Everyone enjoyed the fresh trout and for years thereafter it was said of that vacation, that what we lacked in numbers we more than made up for in size.

Well, there you have it, all the unadorned facts. Mom, Dad, and alas poor David have all since passed on without cathartic disclosure. Before David's death he and I would on rare occasion speak of these events, but always privately and in very hushed tones. Thereafter while accompanying Dad on hikes up Gothics we no longer tarried at the wall overlooking the breeders. Although I never said so to David, I came to feel that we had sullied that spot. I can tell you this, however: the events of that day brought about my conversion from the life of a meat fisherman.

One question does still remain. Will the members of the Ausable Club ever forgive me?

Building Character

It was one of those mid-August days that promised to be hot—a Friday as I recollect. Mom used to like to shop for groceries on Fridays in preparation for Dad's arrival late that night. The day did prove to be very hot—which did not help the familial discord that was brewing.

Mom insisted that Davy and I be responsible for a list of chores around camp. On our arrival each June, she would "publish" the list of chores, some of which were one-time major projects while others were recurring tasks. The list was quite comprehensive, designating the responsible party, frequency, and due dates. On this day we were jointly commanded to mow the lawn around the camp.

Our camp was located on the crest of a hill surrounded by what had been a cow pasture. Once or twice each year, Mom would have

Dewey Duntley mow the meadow with his horse-drawn mower. Dewey obliged as he used the cuttings for hay for the few cows that he kept. Although Dewey's mowing kept most of the meadow neat, Mom was more demanding with respect to the grass immediately around the camp structure. This grooming was assigned to us jointly on a weekly basis.

Our mower, like most of the tools at camp, was a hand-me-down from some friend or family member. It seems that everyone wanted to unload their used and abused stuff on us. Mom, being the frugal Swiss that she was, couldn't resist such gifts.

The machine had to be the first self-propelled power mower made. It was a reel type with a Brigg and Stratton mounted on top. The blades and wheels were driven by separate bicycle chains, both of which would frequently jump their sprockets during operation. The tires, if they ever had treads, were worn as smooth as a baby's posterior. On the grades around the camp the tires would often slip, in some spots requiring both of us to push what was a rather heavy machine. We would take turns returning the slipped chains to their sprockets. We complained a lot—Mom always assured us the experience would "build character."

On this day, over breakfast, we tried to persuade Mom that mowing was not necessary. Davy argued that there had been no rain and very little growth. I repeated something heard from Dad, that it was not good to cut grass too short during periods of hot weather. Mom would have none of it, reminding us how much more difficult it became to mow tall grass. We continued our plaintive whimpering as Mom cleared the table, but she gave no indication that she heard us. In her absence we continued to assure ourselves that mowing was not only unnecessary, at was absolutely unwise. After all, Dad would be upset if we were to cause the lawn to burn. Our commiserating came to an abrupt end when Mom returned and said, "*Now.*" That word, delivered with that inflection, meant the discussion was over.

Ever so slowly we retrieved the mower from the garage, filled the gas tank, and began to mow. Rather than mowing in straight lines, we would follow the contour of the hill. In so doing we avoided some of those wheel-slipping grades, a trick our Uncle Herman had taught us the previous summer. Each of us took a turn operating the mower while the other raked the clippings into little mounds. That day we took frequent breaks to continue our breakfast-table complaints. At one point Mom came to the front porch and demanded that we pick up the pace, as we would shortly be leaving to do the weekly grocery shopping.

On finishing our chore, we went inside where Mom examined our faces and hands to be certain we were presentable for a trip to town. After a quick washing and hair comb, we proceeded to the '37 Chevy, which was parked in the garage. The garage had both a front and smaller rear door. On this day we all entered the garage through the rear door, a decision that would prove to be calamitous.

As usual, Davy and I began to argue who would ride shotgun. By now Mom had had her fill of us and quickly ordered me into the back seat. With the doors closed Mom started the Chevy, put it in reverse, and looking over her shoulder began backing out of the garage. We had not moved more than a few feet when I felt the rear of the car heave into the air and return to the ground with a bounce. As I rose and fell with the car, I heard the crunching sound of breaking metal.

Mom uttered some expletive in her Swiss-German dialect and jumped from the car. We both followed her to discover the remains of the mower. For a brief moment, we all stood there staring at the broken bits and pieces, but quite quickly Davy and I began to laugh. It was the kind of laughter brought on by the sight of someone stumbling; at that age all sorts of mishaps would strike us as humorous. But Mom didn't see the humor. We each received a box on the ears as she stated, "You did this on purpose." We both protested our innocence while she directed the removal of the debris from under and around the rear of the Chevy. Having cleared the debris, Mom ordered both of us into the rear seat.

Our camp was located at a point in North Hudson that was equidistant from Elizabethtown, Port Henry, and Schroon Lake. During various summers, Mom might have shopped at any of these towns, depending on her perception of price or the quality of meats and produce. During this summer she opted to shop in Port Henry.

As a result, leaving camp, we proceeded a few miles south on Route 9 and then East on the Black Brook Road.

The first few miles were traveled in total silence. As we rode along, Davy and I each privately considered our fate. Mom was clearly angry, and independently we came to the conclusion that the negligent party should fess up. "You put the mower in the garage," Davy accused. "No, I didn't, you did," I replied. These exchanges continued for a bit when Mom announced that the bickering should stop, or we would both be left by the side of the road. Now Mom had frequently threatened to leave us by the side of the road, but never had done so before. Once we came close. Riding along busy Route 17 in New Jersey, she ended a squabble between us by removing us from the car and delivering a stern lecture on the side of the road.

For a while, our exchange ceased, but then under our breath we began again. Mouthing our blaming, we began to punctuate our accusations with poking fingers, which escalated into a shoving match. All of a sudden, the Chevy made a hard turn to the right and came to an abrupt stop on the shoulder of the road. Even before the car had fully stopped, Mom shouted, "Out!" We sat for a moment in stunned silence. When she repeated the command, we both got out and stared at her through the open door. "Shut the door," Mom directed. As I pushed the door closed, the Chevy's wheels began to spin. In a cloud of dust and a hail of roadside stones, the Chevy leaped forward. In short order, Mom and the Chevy disappeared around a turn in the Black Brook Road.

For a while, we stood by the roadside, assuring each other that Mom would soon return. "She's trying to scare us," we told each other. But as time passed we came to the realization that Mom was going to Port Henry alone. The reassuring words we spoke at first soon became expressions of indignation. "How could she leave us here? Who would feed us lunch?" Weekly trips to town typically included a cheeseburger lunch in a local eatery. Cheeseburgers were not in the cards today. Mom would be dining alone, and we were stranded on a very desolate stretch of the Black Brook Road.

By now we had ceased standing by the roadside and taken a seat on a nearby fallen tree. Seated there, we began to take stock of our options. We could stay put and wait for Mom to pick us up on the return trip—or we could walk home. Walking really wasn't an option. Mom would surely overtake us at some point en route. All that we would have achieved is needless fatigue and a lecture. Staying put avoided the fatigue, but not the dreaded lecture. How to avoid the lecture? For a brief moment, we considered hitchhiking. However, based on Mom's strong admonition against such activity, the idea was quickly scrapped—besides, there was little if any vehicular traffic on that road. The combative spirit that brought us to this predicament quickly turned collaborative. "We will show her. We won't be left by the roadside."

Although the distance by road to our camp was many miles, as the crow flew it was at most three, perhaps three and one-half miles away. The trip to our present position had taken us south on Route 9 and then northeast on the Black Brook Road. Our present position was due east of the camp, separated by Claybed Mountain. The local geography was very familiar to us. Along with Adirondack trail guides, Dad had purchased a number of coast and geodetic-survey maps. From those maps we had located a number of remote trout ponds. One of the fishing spots we frequented was Twin Ponds, two small beaver ponds on the northern shoulder of Claybed Mountain. On one of our hikes to the ponds, we encountered a pair of fishermen who advised us that that they had come via the Black Brook Road, and from there a short walk up an old lumber road. On previous trips to Port Henry, Davy and I attempted to locate that lumber road, and were fairly certain we had based upon the frequency, which we observed cars and pickups parked at the spot. It was our fortune that Mom had abandoned us a short distance from that spot.

And so it was that we determined to beat Mom home. We would walk to the camp, not along the road, but cross-country.

We set off on a brisk jog and quickly found the logging road we believed would lead us to Twin Ponds. Our pace slowed considerably as the road went up a steep grade and at spots had become heavily overgrown with maple saplings. Despite the slower pace, in less than twenty minutes we cleared a rise, and below us through the trees saw a body of water. Several minutes more, and we were on the shore of one of the Twin Ponds.

From this point, we knew our way home. We gingerly stepped over the beaver dam, which formed the lower of the ponds and ran down a grade along the creek that exited the ponds. At the bottom of the grade, the creek joined the East Mill Flow, a tributary to the Schroon River. The East Mill Flow ran through two large marshes before passing near to our camp. We would not take that route, but instead forded the Flow to reach another lumber track, which would take us more directly, over high ground, to the camp. Another forty-five minutes, and with aching lungs, we reached camp.

Mom was of course nowhere in sight. By our reckoning Mom had finished shopping, had lunch, and was just starting the return trip. We would have lots of time to prepare for her arrival. While jogging home, we had exchanged ideas for the reunion. We would have to portray a relaxed air, demonstrate brotherly camaraderie, as though nothing untoward had occurred. Davy pulled out the hammock while I rolled out the chase lounge. Together we stretched out with glasses of lemonade and copies of *Field and Stream* to await Mom's return.

And wait we did. Long after all the lemonade had been consumed and our backsides had become numb from our supine positions, the Chevy hove into view. If surprised, Mom gave no inkling of it. "Help me with the groceries," she barked. Years later Mom would tell us how worried she had been not to find us by the roadside and how she had driven back and forth on the Black Brook Road looking for us. But on that day Mom would ignore our attempt at smugness.

Once all the groceries had been stowed, Davy and I stood awkwardly about the kitchen, waiting for the other shoe to drop. "Don't just stand there," Mom ordered, "there is more in the trunk." With that, Davy and I walked back to the Chevy while Mom followed. As we opened the trunk, Mom stood on the front porch and observed. Lifting the trunk lid, we found a spanking brand-new mower. Like the old machine it was the reel type, but there the similarity ended. This machine had no engine, it required manpower. We both stood motionless, staring into the trunk as the reality of our new mowing paradigm took hold.

"It has a grass catcher, so you won't have to rake." Mom observed.

"But it doesn't have a motor," I complained.

"No, it doesn't," Mom agreed, "but it will build character."

Hemple Ham

As I have observed before, Dad seemed to experience the Adirondacks in a spiritual way. While not a religious person, the reverential way he spoke of his hiking experiences revealed a very deep, emotional connection with these mountains. As children and later as young adults, Dad would find unending joy in sharing vistas from the High Peaks with Davy and me. Below the tree line he would frequently stop to observe birds or help us learn to identify Adirondack flora and fauna. Occasionally he would stop walking and ask us to "listen." The sounds of birds, rushing water, or wind in the trees seemed to provide him an emotional high.

While Mom often joined Dad on hikes, she did not find the same spiritual connection with the mountains. Mom, born in Switzerland, had been raised a Lutheran. She considered herself a devoutly religious person, although she seemed forever in search of a satisfying way to express her religious devotion. Her search led her to a succession of Protestant denominations, including several months of study with a group of Jehovah's Witnesses. In later life, Davy and I would kid Mom about joining the "Religion of the Month Club."

Dad was very understanding of Mom's search for spiritual solace but absolutely refused to attend services with her. "I find my religion in nature," he would tell her. "The woods and mountains are my chapel. If there is a God, that's where I can be close to him." Davy and I were not as fortunate. As children, we experienced numerous Sunday schools as Mom made her way from one denomination to another. We would often complain to Dad that we didn't want to attend Sunday school, but he insisted that we accompany our mother. Our only respite came for us during the summer months when we retreated to camp for the entire summer, and even Mom took a respite from church services. The nearest church to our camp was serviced sporadically by an itinerant minister; other options were far too distant.

I was perhaps thirteen years old when Mom joined the local Baptist church in New Jersey. At that age I didn't want to attend Sunday school with younger children, and so Mom took me with her to the regular services. The congregation was an eclectic group, including numerous African Americans. The services were quite different from those I had witnessed in other churches, with lively music and rousing animation among both the choir and worshipers during song. Often I found myself stirred to swing in rhythm with the rest of the congregation, and soon I had memorized most of the music. This music was far different from the difficult-to-sing hymns sung at the Presbyterian church. The music was invigorating.

On one occasion, Mom took me to an evening service, one which featured a traveling evangelist. As we approached the church the sounds of song could be heard from blocks away, far louder than was customary for the choir. As we entered the sanctuary, it became clear why the decibel level had increased. In addition to the usual choir, the evangelist had brought a second far-larger choir and a ten-piece band. The building shook, and I became quite excited by what might come next. In part, my excitement stemmed from the fact that I didn't know what an evangelist was or did. Mom and I found a good place to sit; I was seated directly on the center aisle. Several pews ahead, I saw Charlie Hemple and his parents. Charlie was a classmate whose parents owned a delicatessen frequented by my parents.

The music continued until all the seats were filled and the rear and side aisles crowded with standees. As the pastor approached the pulpit, the music came to an end. He offered a prayer and then introduced the guest of the evening, Jack Wyrtzen. Mr. Wyrtzen didn't look like a preacher. He didn't wear the black garb and white collar worn by our minister. He wore ordinary chino pants and a plaid short-sleeved shirt. He wore gold-rimmed glasses and carried a Bible.

Following the introduction, the Pastor retired to a seat at the side, and Mr. Wyrtzen stepped into the center of the church announcing that he would lead all in song. The band played the introductory bars to "What a Friend We Have in Jesus" and were joined by both choirs, the congregation, and Mr. Wyrtzen. I was surprised that despite the volume of hundreds of voices, without a microphone Mr. Wyrtzen's voice was clearly discernable above all others.

After singing all verses, Mr. Wyrtzen signaled with a slow downward motion of outstretched arms for the choirs and band to be seated. He began to speak, and as he did so he walked about the church. As he spoke he would stop beside a pew and look directly into the eyes of those seated there, occasionally laying a hand on a head or shoulder. As he addressed the congregation he would occasionally read from his Bible. The message was simple: we were all sinners, and the only way to heaven was to accept Jesus Christ as your personal savior. As he spoke, his voice would rise and fall. At times it was so loud that I would recoil, at other times it was but an audible whisper. At one point he stopped beside me and, looking me directly in the eyes, proclaimed that we are not only burdened with original sin, but as weak mortals we are doomed to sin throughout our lives. The message seemed aimed at me, and I scrunched down in the pew.

After a while Mr. Wyrtzen introduced a number of people who "gave witness" to their conversion to Jesus Christ. Most were young people, but one older gentleman professed to be a former alcoholic. Each would recall the moment of conversion and relate how that event positively affected their lives. As their stories were told, the congregation would punctuate the telling with "glory be" and "hallelujah." The former alcoholic's tale drew the most comment from the congregation. After each "witness," Mr. Wyrtzen would lead the choirs in rousing song. By now the event was having a deep emotional impact upon me.

And so it was that when Mr. Wyrtzen asked for members of the congregation to come forward and be "saved," I did. I was one of perhaps a dozen my age, including Charlie Hemple. As the event concluded, Mr. Wyrtzen announced that he had founded a Bible camp for young people. It was located on an island in Schroon Lake in the Adirondacks. He urged all parents to send their children—Mom was given a pamphlet with all the particulars.

On the way home, Mom told me how happy and proud of me she was. When we returned to the house, Dad was seated in his comfortable chair reading the *New York Times*. Mom announced to him that I had been "saved." A quizzical expression betrayed any understanding of the evening's event. As Mom explained, the expression quickly turned bemused. The following Sunday, Charlie Hemple and I were baptized in a huge tank of water beneath the floor of the sanctuary, just forward of the pulpit.

Charlie had been a classmate ever since we moved to Middletown, New Jersey. He was quite big for his age, a good student, but the kind of know-it-all that all the kids quickly got to dislike. He wasn't a bad athlete and because of his size could hit a softball a fair distance. This ability assured that he would quickly be chosen to field a team when softball was played at recess or during gym class. I didn't consider him a friend, but for some reason we were frequently chosen to play on the same softball team. During a recess game shortly after our baptism I was playing third base, and he shortstop, when he commented, "Looks like we are going to the Word of Life Camp together." I professed ignorance. "Our moms are planning it," he advised.

That afternoon I rushed home to quiz Mom. Yes indeed she had discussed the matter with Mrs. Hemple while making some purchases at the delicatessen. Mom had mentioned that our camp was a few miles north of Schroon Lake, the location of Mr. Wyrtzen's Bible camp. They apparently agreed that it would be "nice if the boys could attend together." I protested that we weren't friends, but Mom observed that Charlie and I had together experienced a life-changing event that we should build upon at Mr. Wyrtzen's Bible camp. "Years from now you will both look back at this as a milestone in the development of your spiritual life." It was ultimately decided that Dad would take his vacation the last two weeks of July. Dad would bring Charlie with him, and Charlie and I would spend the first week at the Word of Life camp. After camp Charlie would spend a few days with our family and then return to his family via a Trailways bus.

We arrived at camp in early June—Mom, Davy, and I—for the duration of the summer. Dad arrived late Friday nights for the weekend, sometimes taking an extra day. Mid-July he arrived with Charlie in tow. As usual he arrived well after midnight. Most times the barking of our dog would rouse us, as it did on the night of Charlie's arrival. I greeted Charlie in a half-sleep stupor as he struggled into camp with a duffel bag and what appeared to be a very heavy shopping bag. He handed the bag to Mom, explaining it was a gift from the delicatessen. From the bag Mom pulled the largest canned ham I have ever seen—it must have weighed twenty pounds. Mom thanked him and we all retired.

As usual Davy and I were up with the light of dawn. Charlie was having some trouble following us to the breakfast table given the unaccustomed 350-mile nighttime trek he just underwent. I was helping Mom with breakfast while Davy was whining about not being able to go to the Word of Life camp. Mom explained that he was too young, and besides, he hadn't been saved yet. "Perhaps you can go next year." We had a great breakfast that included grilled ham—the ham Charlie brought. When Mom first opened the can, my stomach turned at the sight of the gelatinous covering of the meat. But Mom quickly removed it and once grilled we all again thanked Charlie for his family's gift.

Mom had earlier received instructions from Mr. Wyrtzen's staff regarding our arrival at Word of Life. We were expected to report at noon that Saturday at a dock just off Route 9 in Schroon Lake. Our duffel had been packed with the prescribed and appropriately labeled items of clothing, a Bible, a notebook, and a pen. As we stood on the dock, Davy was still complaining about being excluded. Dad tried to assure him that he would have a good time hiking with him. "But they are going to an island," he protested. As beautiful as the location of our camp was, it wasn't on water—something Davy and I both longed for. Like most kids our age, we were drawn to water and the activities it offered. At the appointed hour, a boat arrived and Charlie and I were checked in together with several other arrivals, some of them girls our age. I kissed Mom goodbye and set sail for Bible camp.

We were ferried to the island on a covered launch, which was docked in a boathouse. Previously, while grocery shopping with Mom in Schroon Lake Village, I had often seen this launch ply its way back and forth to the island. I then envied those unseen passengers who made that crossing; now I had joined them.

On disembarking, we were greeted by our counselor, a college student whose name I have long since forgotten. He assisted us in taking our duffel to a dormitory, which housed several dozen boys our age. After unpacking and given an orientation of the dormitory, we joined numerous other campers in the dining hall for lunch and an address by Mr. Wyrtzen himself. He described what camp life would be like and that he hoped that as a result we would become "better witnesses for the word of God." His words and the forceful way he delivered them brought back some of the same emotions I had experienced the night of my conversion. He told us we would be divided into groups to study specific books of the Bible. Study sessions were scheduled for both morning and afternoon. Between the afternoon session and the evening meal, recreational activities such as swimming and canoeing were scheduled. After the evening meal, we would receive instruction in how to lead a Christian life, followed by time to prepare for the next day's lessons.

Charlie and I were placed in a group of perhaps forty and charged with the study of the book of Daniel, which over the course of the ensuing week was dissected and analyzed line by line. As he had done in his secular studies, Charlie immersed himself in the topic and strove to be the first to respond to any question posed by the instructor. For me the time dragged by very slowly, while the time scheduled for recreation was far too short and restricted by camp rules. During the Daniel lectures, I found myself gazing out the window and longing to be with Dad and Davy hiking up the Ridge Trail.

Evening sessions were less formal, usually segregated by sex and focused on how to live a good Christian life. Several sessions were devoted to the evangelical need to spread the word of God. Charlie was especially taken by this mission and the exhortation to pursue even the most hardened sinner. One evening the topic was chastity before marriage and concluded with the evils of masturbation and how to avoid the temptation.

Walking back to the dormitory, Charlie announced his new mission in life—to convert Mickey Lewis. Now, Mickey Lewis was a classmate of ours who was far more physically developed than the rest of the boys in our class. I don't know whether he was left behind in lower grades or some hormonal anomaly required him to shave daily. In any event, Mickey didn't have our prepubescent appearance and would regale us with his sexual exploits at every opportunity. Gym-class locker-room encounters provided him with an extraordinary platform from which to report his dalliances. I cautioned Charlie that remonstrance against masturbation would have little impact upon Mickey and suggested that he find a softer first target. Charlie responded with some Biblical quotation that even the worst of sinners can find salvation.

The week finally came to an end, and we made the reverse trip by launch to the mainland. Charlie engaged in an enthusiastic conversation with Mom on the trip to camp. Mom, whether by reason of her studies with the Jehovah's Witnesses or otherwise, was able to engage Charlie in his discussion of Daniel. After learning that I did not have time to fish, Davy lost interest in our Word of Life venture. Dad drove silently to camp.

Whether he had taken my advice not to pursue Mickey Lewis as his first conquest or he had become anxious to begin his evangelical career, by suppertime it was clear that Dad had become Charlie's first target. I believe he may have formulated the idea when Dad began to help himself to the mashed potatoes before Charlie was able to offer grace. I am not certain whether grace was a part of Charlie's family tradition, Despite Mom's piety, it certainly wasn't a part of ours. However, at Bible camp Charlie had been rewarded for his outstanding contribution to the Daniel study group by being selected to offer grace one breakfast. He prepared an eloquent offering that he repeated that evening, with an embellishment that implored the almighty to assist in the conversion of all the assembled. While Dad did not bow his head or fold his hands, he did suspend the serving of mashed potatoes.

Charlie was unrelenting in his attempt to convert Dad. While Dad was always more than willing to engage young people in intellectual discussion, he did his best to convey to Charlie, in a polite way, that he was not interested in a discussion of the hereafter or a "personal relationship with Christ."

The following day Dad had planned a hike up Noonmark, a hike he often used to introduce novice guests to the Adirondacks. Over breakfast Charlie continued to pursue Dad. Once again Dad did his best to avoid engaging Charlie in discussion. After breakfast, Mom was preparing sandwiches for the hike—ham sandwiches. While much reduced in size, Charlie's gift had yet to be totally consumed. As she prepared our lunch, I overheard Dad ask her what arrangements she had made to return Charlie to his parents. Mom told Dad that she had a Trailways ticket for Charlie's return the following day. Charlie would have to be taken to Hosley's General Store, the only place in North Hudson where the bus could be stopped on demand. Once aboard the bus, Dad was to call Charlie's Mom with his expected time of arrival in Newark, New Jersey.

Before heading to the Noonmark trailhead, Dad drove to Hosley's General Store. We all followed Dad into the store; Davy and I liked to look at the hunting and fishing gear on display. Dad asked Mr. Hosley if he would hail the bus scheduled to pass through town midmorning the following day. Mr. Hosley consulted his bus schedule, advised Dad of the arrival time, and explained that he would set out at the roadside a milk can into which he would insert a red flag on a pole. This was his signal to the bus driver to stop.

The hike up Noonmark was unlike any other I had taken with Dad. Typically, Dad would stay close to guests; he loved the role of Adirondack guide. On that day there was none of the usual banter, as Dad set a fast pace remaining well ahead of Charlie all the way to the summit. At the summit we encountered another group of hikers who

Dad engaged in endless conversation. On any other occasion, Dad would have gathered us together to identify each of the visible peaks. In this fashion, he avoided Charlie throughout the day, retiring early that evening.

The following morning, shortly after the breakfast table was cleared, Dad began to urge Charlie to pack his duffel. Mom observed that there was still plenty of time to get Charlie down to Hosley's, but Dad insisted he didn't want to take any chances and miss the bus. With much time to spare, Dad loaded Charlie's gear in the family station wagon. Mom bid Charlie goodbye, and Davy and I joined Dad on the trip to Hosley's.

It only took a few minutes to reach the store, and as we did Dad wondered aloud why Mr. Hosley hadn't put out the milk can and flag. I followed Dad into the store while Charlie and Davy retrieved the duffel bag from the back of the wagon. Inside the store Dad asked Mr. Hosley why the signal flag hadn't been placed by the road-side. "No use," he replied. "Ten, maybe fifteen minutes ago I was out pumping gas when the bus came through here. Surprised me—had no time to flag him down. They must have changed the schedule, or else he was way ahead of schedule." Dad first inquired when the next bus was expected. When told there were only two each day, the second passing through during the early evening hours, he then asked where the next bus stop was. Mr. Hosley advised that there was usually a scheduled stop at the Pitkin Restaurant in Schroon Lake.

Dad ran from the store, grabbed Charlie's duffel where it had been dropped, and threw it back into the wagon. "Boys, get into the car," he commanded. With barely time to close the doors, Dad spun the wagon around and headed for Schroon Lake. Now Mom had always complained that Dad drove too fast, but I never had known him to drive as fast as he did that day, certainly never on twisting and turning Route 9. When younger Davy and I had hung over the seat behind Dad and urged him to "go fifty." When the speedometer needle hit fifty or occasionally fifty-five, we would give a cheer, and Mom would give Dad one of her looks. That day Davy sat behind Dad and, pointing over his shoulder, would mouth "sixty-five" or "seventy."

We flew past the tourist cabins at the outskirts of Schroon Lake, past the Central School, and as Pitkins came into view there was no sign of a bus. Dad made an abrupt stop in front of the restaurant and, commanding that we remain in the car, ran into the restaurant. In moments he returned and without a word rapidly shifted through the gears until we were again traveling well above his customary speed. "Where are we going?" I inquired. "The Chester Town bus stop" was his reply.

During those days, before the Northway had been constructed, Dad knew every shortcut between camp and home. One such shortcut involved a secondary road between Pottersville and Chester Town. Much of that road was rough and unpaved, and Dad usually reduced his speed to spare both the vehicle and its occupants. That day we churned up huge clouds of dust as we and the wagon chattered our way to Chester Town.

As we left the shortcut and again merged with Route 9, we saw a Trailways bus ahead of us. We followed the bus to its Chester Town stop and Dad pulled the wagon alongside the bus in a way so that it couldn't leave, were such the driver's wish. Dad retrieved the duffel bag and escorted Charlie to the door of the bus where he conversed with the driver while he gave him Charlie's ticket. Davy and I followed and said our goodbyes to Charlie. Dad moved the wagon, and we all stood by until the bus pulled out and drove out of sight.

The drive back to camp was leisurely; actually, Dad drove at a pace slower then was customary for him—almost as though he was making amends for his earlier excesses. At first none of us spoke. I was feeling somewhat embarrassed for the grief Charlie had given Dad. I had not come to Dad's aid. I had said nothing to Charlie. Did Dad think I shared Charlie's views? In fact, my thoughts about religion were becoming very confused. How could a man like my dad, a dad who took me hiking, who could identify every living plant and tree, who professed that living with nature was his religion, how could such a man be damned to hell because he didn't accept Jesus Christ as his personal savior? I had nearly put those thoughts out of my mind when we passed the Word of Life dock where just a few days earlier Charlie and I had left Bible camp behind.

Dad broke the silence and my musing. "Well, boys, what do you want to do tomorrow, fishing or a climb up Gothics with me?" Knowing that Davy might want to fish, I quickly responded, "I'll hike with you."

When we arrived at camp Mom had set lunch out on the porch table. As we walked up the porch steps she said, "I thought you got lost. You have been gone for hours. Where have you been?"

Davy recounted the chase to Chester Town in minute detail: "You should've seen Dad—we hit eighty on the flats outside Schroon Lake."

Mom gave Dad one of her looks and said, "What will the Hemples think?"

Dad looked her in the face and said, "I would have chased that bus to Albany if I had to."

Once seated for lunch, Dad asked, "Well, Steve, will you be going to Word of Life next year?"

"No, I don't think so," I responded.

Smiling broadly, Dad looked at Mom and said, "Please pass me a piece of that Hemple Ham."

Blue Tones over Lake
Tear of the Clouds

B y now you know that my father loved to scale the High Peaks—he lived for that experience. Although the rest of the family did enjoy joining him on the trail, we clearly did not get the same enjoyment from the experience as he did. Dad didn't simply do it as a change of pace or for the exercise, or the solace of the woods; he did it for all those reasons, and then some we will never know or understand. Often he would abruptly stop on the trail and ask us to listen. Sometimes he would inquire what we had heard. Other times, after several minutes of silence, he would simply continue walking without commenting on the sound of the flicker, the rush of water over stones, or simply the wind in the trees we had stopped to appreciate.

Although Dad would hike alone, he definitely preferred to have company. The entire family was urged to join him on every hike he took, but if fishing drew Davy and me to the Ausable and Mom to chores around the camp, Dad was off on his own. Not infrequently Dad brought coworkers from his office or neighbors from home to camp as hiking companions. Some of those draftees became converts and often returned for other hiking adventures. More frequently they simply thanked Dad for the experience and never returned again.

That is not to say that as a family we did not make frequent and very enjoyable hikes together. One of the most memorable was our three-day trek from Elk Lake to St. Huberts, over Mt. Marcy and Sawteeth. That was a hike of more than twenty-five miles, with backpacks, over some very tough terrain. The first day took us over long stretches of wet ground to the Panther Gorge Lean-to at the base of Marcy, a desolate stretch of trail where we saw no one else. On one particularly swampy section traversed by a corduroy trail, Mom slipped and her pack caused her to lose balance and fall into the soup. Davy and I fell into fits of hysterical laughter; it's strange how young teenagers can find humor in such mishaps. On the second day we left gear at the lean-to, scaled Marcy, and returned for supper and sleep. On the third and final day, we first hiked to a point near the foot of Upper Ausable Lake to a very scenic spot on Shanty Brook. As it turned out, we relaxed there far too long. Mom prepared lunch with the last of our provisions. We had spiced ham from a can on crackers with an assortment of dried fruits and nuts. Several Ausable Club members wandered by, and as it was his custom, Dad engaged them in endless conversation. It had to be close to 4:00 p.m. when we finally hit the trail again. Sawteeth proved an apt name for a mountain Dad had not previously climbed. After ascending and descending several of the teeth, it became clear that we would not reach St. Huberts until well after dark. As we began the final descent, we broke out flashlights and very slowly picked our way down to the Lake Road. As we did, the batteries finally failed. Luckily, the Lake Road is wide and the night was bright with stars. Davy and I were starved. I still remember lying on a green on the golf course eating a

Hershey bar I had purchased from the night clerk at the St. Huberts Lodge, while Dad called Norm Clark to pick us up.

As memorable as that hike was, nothing can compare with another hike that Davy and I took with Dad up Marcy. For many years, Dad said he wanted to see sunrise from Marcy. Quite often he pondered which route would be the most expeditious to arrive at that critical moment. The Elk route was obviously out of the question. But for similar reasons, both the Johns Brook and Van Hoevenberg approaches were problematic. Davy and I were both in our very late teens when Dad decided to make the approach via Avalanche Pass to Four Corners and Lake Tear of the Clouds. In those days the state still permitted lean-tos at higher elevations such as Lake Tear of the Clouds. We would hike to that lean-to and the next morning scramble up the remaining open ledge to catch the first sun's rays as they came over the Green Mountains of Vermont.

For those unfamiliar with Adirondack geography or history, Lake Tear of the Clouds is a tiny gem of a lake, high up on the southern shoulder and very close to the summit of Mt. Marcy, the state's highest peak. The appellation *lake* is misleading as this is a very small body of water. That little lake is also the most northern source of the Hudson River, and the spot where Teddy Roosevelt first learned that Harding had died and he had become president of the United States.

And so it was that Dad, Davy, and I arrived late one summer afternoon at the lean-to on the shore of Lake Tear of the Clouds. The lean-to was positioned on the southerly shore facing the bald summit of Marcy; it was an impressive sight. The sun had already begun to set, and Dad unrolled the sleeping bags while Davy and I collected wood and began a cooking fire in the stone enclosure at the front of the lean-to. Once the flames receded a bit, Dad unpacked the cooking gear, which included a number of nested pots, pans, and tin dishes. These vessels, together with utensils and two pot holders, were stored for travel in a canvas bag. The pot holders, actually padded gloves, would play a central role that evening. The sun was fast setting, casting a golden glow on the rocky summit of Marcy as Dad began cooking our meal.

Now you must know that neither Davy nor I ever heard a foul word from the mouth of our father. Although the use of gratuitous profanity had not in the late 1950s reached the proportions commonplace in this century, both Davy and I had heard our fair share in school and elsewhere. Neither of us would have dared to use profanity at home, and the thought that Dad might do so was beyond belief.

As Dad prepared dinner, we soon began to hear voices from the trail below. As the voices came nearer, Dad instructed that we should move our sleeping bags to one side to make room for the arriving hikers. As we did so, a party of three young men, perhaps in their late twenties, approached the lean-to. Dad greeted them warmly and motioned to the space we had cleared for them in the lean-to. As our evening guests unpacked, they let fly with a series of F-bombs. As their conversation continued, it seemed like every sentence was punctuated with that word. Davy and I gave each other sideways glances, both wondering how Dad was dealing with such a barrage of blue language. Neither of us had ever been with Dad when others in such close proximity used such language, much less in this environment for which he held such reverence.

Our guests continued their blue banter for what seemed an eternity. All the while Dad continued silently making dinner. Finally there was pause in their conversation. Standing next to Dad, I could hear him take a deep breath and in an exceptionally load and emphatic voice say to me, "Steve hand me that fuuucccking pot holder." It took a moment, but almost in unison Davy and I fell into fits of hysterical laughter. Dad turned to take the pot holder from my shaking hand, a big grin on his face. It worked—the F-bombs abated for the evening.

The next morning, we left the lean-to in the dim predawn light, leaving our guests sound asleep. We made the summit just as the sun's rays were breaking over the mountains to the East. Dad was in his element, having stricken a long sought-after item from his Adirondack bucket list. Davy and I were still laughing, as we did for years later, when we would ask one another to "pass that *blankety-blank* pot holder."

Lucky Break

I had just graduated from law school and was clerking for a superior court judge when one day my former wife came home from work and told me that we had been invited to join her boss and his wife for the upcoming, long Fourth of July weekend. She told me that we would be staying with a cousin of her boss's wife, who owned a camp on Lake Placid—a camp that only had boat access. We had made previous plans for that weekend, plans that I immediately threw out the window.

Throughout our youth, Brother Davy and I fished many lakes in the northeastern corner of the Adirondacks. Some lakes we fished frequently; Lake Placid we fished but once when we were in our late teens. Although that lake was fished only once, that trip stuck in my memory like no other. It wasn't the fish that we caught that stoked my memory, but rather the gorgeous natural setting and impressive

Adirondack-style camps and boathouses along the waterfront. The chance to stay at one of those camps could not be missed.

*****

As I have recounted many times before, while Davy and I loved to fish, Dad loved to climb the High Peaks. As often as we could, Davy and I would look for fishing opportunities that might accompany one of Dad's hiking trips. Occasionally that meant joining Dad with light fishing gear, if the planned trail would intersect with a stream or pond of interest. Many times it simply meant that we would be dropped off at some location along Dad's drive to a trailhead. Our only fishing trip to Lake Placid occurred in an unusual way.

As usual Mom, Davy, and I had stayed at camp all summer long, while Dad came on weekends—often with friends or coworkers for a hike. One weekend he told us that on the following weekend he would be bringing a few coworkers who wanted to climb Whiteface Mountain. He told us this while sitting on the front porch with the Adirondack Mountain Club's trail map on his lap. Hoping for an accompanying fishing opportunity, Davy and I looked over his shoulders.

Dad began running his fingers over two trails leading to the summit of Whiteface. Both had trailheads on roadways, but one ran for some distance to a remote corner on the shore of Lake Placid before ascending the peak. Seeing an opportunity to fish Lake Placid, I pointed to the spot where the trail touched the lake and said, "Dad, you can rent a boat for my outboard, and I will get you there—that's a shorter hike."

"I don't know if you can rent boats on Lake Placid," he responded as he opened the club's trail guide. After reading a bit, he acknowledged that the club considered that shoreline location a trailhead, and that a dock made it accessible. Turning to Mom, I asked, "Can't we grocery shop in Lake Placid this week and try to find a boat livery?"

Mom agreed and that week Davy and I joined her as she grocery shopped in Lake Placid. At the Grand Union checkout she inquired where she might find boats for rent. The clerk said she was not certain if boats were available for rent, but that we should try a marina called George and Bliss. After loading the groceries in our 1937 Chevy, following the clerk's directions Mom drove a short distance out of town to George and Bliss.

The marina was located on the southeasterly corner of Lake Placid, a location from which there was a magnificent view of Whiteface Mountain on the far end of the lake. The marina had numerous slips, many of them covered, housing gorgeous mahogany inboard boats. At first we just wandered about taking in the scenery and marveling over the beautiful Chris-Crafts, Hacker-Crafts, and Garwoods. As we did so, Mom was looking for someone to speak with, but except for us no one was about. It had just turned noon, and Mom noted that everyone might be at lunch. She suggested that we get some lunch and return later. As we began to return to the car, I pointed to a large barn-like shed at the far end of the docks. I suggested that we go there first.

The shed had a large open door facing a long open slip, over which hung a large I-beam that protruded from inside the shed. As we entered the shed, we observed a large inboard hanging from that I-beam with dozens of other beautifully finished wooden boats lining the walls on cradles. At the rear of the shed was a door with a window. While the interior of the shed was not illuminated, a beam of electric light shone through that door window. We approached the door and peered through the window, where we observed a shop in the middle of which stood a wooden boat on a cradle that had been stripped of its hardware and varnish. Along one of the shop walls sat three men eating sandwiches, one of whom caught our eye and came to the door.

"Can I help you?" he asked.

"We would like to rent a boat," Mom responded.

"We don't rent rowboats."

"We don't want a rowboat, my son has an outboard motor."

"How many horsepower?"

"It's an Elgin 7.5," I responded.

With that he waved his hand to follow him as he walked through the large open door back out onto the docks. Several slips out into the lake, he stopped and pointed to a square-ended aluminum boat about fourteen feet long. "That's the only boat we have that will work with that motor—if you like it, go fetch the motor."

With that Mom explained that we would need it all day the following Saturday to travel to the Whiteface trailhead. She further explained that we would want to take the boat sometime between 6:00 and 7:00 a.m.

"Nobody will be here at that time, but you can pay now and take it early Saturday."

While Mom went off to pay for the boat, Davy and I more closely examined it—in fact we climbed into it. Although it was square-ended, the bow end was more narrow with a small deck. It had three seats, one being a more narrow one at the bow. Until now, Davy and I had only rented slow-moving, heavy wooden rowboats on our fishing trips. On the way home, I told Mom that my motor could push that boat much faster.

As usual, Dad arrived late on Friday night. Customarily, Davy and I would be asleep on his arrival, but that night we waited up to tell him about the boat. Dad arrived with two coworkers, two really big guys. After listening a bit he said, "I hope it's big enough for all of us."

Mom piped up, "It's only you guys and the boys, I am staying at camp."

Early next morning, while Mom prepared breakfast, Davy and I loaded our fishing gear, the Elgin and a gas can in the back of Dad's station wagon. On the way to the lake, Davy and I engaged in a discussion with Dad's coworkers regarding the boat trip. One of them, holding the Adirondack Mountain Club's trail map, said, "Looks like a long boat trip, three, maybe four miles—that motor back there is kind of small. How long do you think the trip will take?" I assured him that the boat was a light, flat-bottomed aluminum boat that my motor could push pretty fast. But once we arrived at the marina, the concern for the boat trip changed. "That's a pretty small boat for five people," commented Dad.

"There are enough seats," I commented.

"Sure, but can it hold the weight?" he responded.

Dad's coworkers, both humorous guys, began poking fun at Dad. "Get in the boat, Carl, take your shoes off first if you think it will sink."

Dad and I sat on the rear seat, me at the motor controls, the coworkers on the next seat, Davy in the bow. It was a beautiful morning, the sky was cloudless and like its name, the lake's waters were placid. As we left the docks I fully opened the throttle. Contrary to my expectation the boat didn't get up on a plane; Dad's concern about weight was having an effect on speed. The boat plowed along, pushing a large wake from its bow as we slowly made our way through a very calm and silent body of water. Soon Dad's coworkers stopped making jokes and began to comment on the surrounding beauty. Whiteface Mountain became evermore impressive as we moved up the lake. At one point we passed an immense cliff at the very edge of the lake, which I later learned was known as Pulpit Rock. It took better than half an hour to reach the trailhead dock, during which time we didn't see one other boat.

As Dad and his coworkers climbed onto the dock, he cautioned me to be sure to be in the vicinity of the dock starting at two o'clock and to retain sufficient gas for the return trip. I assured him I would do so as Davy, and I took off in a boat that now moved much more rapidly.

Although we spent some time fishing, more time was spent slowly cruising along the mainland and island shorelines gawking at impressive rustic camps and boathouses. Many of the boathouses were filled with beautiful wooden boats, the type we had seen earlier in the week at the George and Bliss Marina. Whenever we saw such boats, we would pass a bit closer to read the gold leaf names on the transoms. Some obviously were family based, but many had Adirondack references or were humorous. As the morning wore on, we encountered a number of such boats out on the lake. All emitted a deep and powerful exhaust tone, while some, depending on their speed, also sent out a wake that bounced us about.

As two o'clock approached, we returned to the bay where the trailhead dock was located. By that time a westerly breeze had arisen, and somewhat of a chop began to form on the lake. However, that bay, with no camps on the shoreline, was quiet, sheltered, and calm. We spent some time fishing and caught several smallmouth bass when we spotted Dad standing on the dock.

I brought the boat alongside the dock, and Dad and his coworkers climbed in. As they did, the coworkers engaged Dad in what appeared to have been a continuous heckling about the "remote Adirondack high peak" they had climbed. Comments were made that Mom didn't have to make sandwiches, given the restaurant at the summit and that women in high heels hadn't been expected. The joking ended abruptly as we left the bay.

The wind had increased and what had been a chop now became small whitecaps that impacted the boat just to the starboard of the bow. The wind and waves generated a spray that hit those seated toward the front, while further slowing the speed of the boat and making steering more difficult. To make matters worse, we encountered several inboards that sent out large wakes. Each time one passed us, I turned the boat into the wake. One inboard sent out such a huge wake that some of it came over the deck and left our feet in at least an inch of water. Dad broke out two tin cups from his knapsack, and he and a coworker began bailing.

The trip back took considerably longer and provided Dad's coworkers with material for jovial comments during the car ride back to camp. That joviality continued throughout dinner and even later as I helped Mom by drying dishes. We could hear their comments and laughter coming from the front porch as Mom leaned over and in a soft voice suggested that the day's experience must have been terrible for me. I was quick to assure her that the day was great. I had always wished that our family camp would abut a body of water, and that day's experience reinforced the desire for all time.

My memory of that day followed me for years and left me with anticipation for that Fourth of July weekend.

*****

My former wife's boss was Peter and his wife Debbie. Both were close to, and well knew the extraordinarily strange personality of her cousin, our host Dick Gruen. Peter had offered to drive us to Lake Placid and did so in his 1966 VW Microbus. Peter drove, and I rode shotgun as our wives chatted in the second seat. As we drove North, Peter began to tell me of his encounters with Debbie's cousin.

Peter's description of Gruen often caused me to express disbelief, only to prompt Debbie to interrupt her conversation and confirm Peter's comment. Gruen had owned a store in Livingston, New Jersey, known as the "Lamp Doctor." He converted antique gas and kerosene lamps to electric use and replaced antique lamp shade covers. His store was overflowing with broken lamps and shades, and customers had to walk through narrow aisles between such debris to find him. Despite the condition of his store, Gruen was successful enough so that he was able to close the business and spend each summer at Lake Placid. Once he arrived, Peter said he would cook a pot of soup, which over the course of the summer would evolve as more water and various ingredients were added. Once again Debbie interrupted by advising us that we would shop for food before crossing the lake; she didn't want to eat the soup. As we drew nearer to Lake Placid, I became convinced that I would be meeting an extraordinarily strange individual.

As we approached the village of Lake Placid, Peter told me that Gruen did not have a phone at his camp, but that Gruen had called him from town earlier in the week and was told we would arrive around three. We arrived considerably earlier and stopped in the village for lunch. Following lunch and a trip to the Grand Union, we drove to the George and Bliss Marina, the same marina I had departed from some twelve years earlier. We removed our gear and groceries from the Microbus, and followed Peter out to a covered slip with an engraved wooden sign "Gruen."

As we waited for Gruen to arrive, Peter and I walked around the marina looking at the various craft. Although I saw a number of classic wooden inboards, there were far fewer than I had seen the last time I was at George and Bliss. Now I saw more aluminum and a few fiberglass boats, some inboards, but many outboards. I commented on that change to Peter, who advised me that Gruen would be picking us up in an antique Chris-Craft.

As we returned to Gruen's slip, Peter advised us that he thought he could see Gruen's boat arriving. In the distance I saw a wooden inboard approaching the marina. As it drew nearer, I saw that it was an impressive, very lengthy craft, one with two forward cockpits, a long engine hatch, and a rear cockpit. As it grew even closer, I got to observe the man behind the wheel, the man I shortly would be introduced to as Dick Gruen.

As he pulled into the slip I saw a pale-faced individual, one wearing frameless glasses and a broad-brimmed, black, Pappy Parker hat. The forward brim of the hat was secured against the crown with what appeared to be a large chicken bone. As he climbed out of the boat I observed a tall man, somewhat overweight and obviously without a good sense of balance. He greeted Peter with a deep baritone voice.

Peter introduced us, after which we began to place our gear and groceries in the boat. As we did so, I began to more closely examine the craft. Although it was probably the most impressive wooden inboard I had ever seen, it certainly wasn't in the best of shape. The varnished finish was quite dull, there were chips and gouges in the decking, and on the starboard siding there was a large v-shaped replacement of planking that had not been finished. Across the transom was the faded gold leaf name *Columbia*. Once our gear was aboard, Peter climbed into the rear cockpit and suggested that I sit with Gruen up front while our wives sit in the second cockpit.

Once aboard, Gruen pushed a button on the dashboard, starting the engine with a deep roar. He then pulled back on a large chrome lever that stuck through the floorboard between us, causing a grinding noise as we slowly backed out of the slip. He then began to turn the boat out into the lake by rotating a most unusual steering wheel. The rim was constructed of wood with five wide brass spokes. The rim wasn't perfectly round as the wood between each of the spokes was irregularly shaped. At the center of the wheel was a small lever that I quickly realized was the accelerator. On the dashboard was an engraved brass plaque with the name "Chris Smith and Sons.".

As we crossed the lake, Gruen and I began a discussion, at first about the boat. I told him that Peter had stated that he would be picking us up in a Chris-Craft. Pointing to the plaque he advised me the boat had been built in 1929, well before Chris Smith named his company Chris-Craft. When asked about the v-shaped unfinished planking, he told me that he had recently acquired the boat from someone who one evening had left it unsecured. It had drifted out into the lake where it was struck by another boat. He expressed joy that the accident hadn't totally destroyed the boat and gave him the opportunity to acquire it for a reasonable sum. He assured me the vessel would be refinished that winter.

We continued across the lake at a slow speed when our conversation abruptly changed as we passed a very large white vessel. "That's the *Doris*, a tour boat George and Bliss sends around the lake a least a dozen times a day," he explained. He went on to complain about it and two other smaller tour boats that frequently past close to his camp, putting out a large wake and loudspeaker noise.

At this point, we had traveled a distance up the eastern side of the lake and passed through a strait between the mainland and an island entering the western side of the lake. As we passed through the strait, he pointed to a camp he said was Kate Smith's. I expressed surprise, and he assured me that Kate had summered at Lake Placid for many years and had transmitted her weekly radio program from that very camp.

As we entered the westerly side of the lake, he turned the craft to the north and began to tell me about the history of his camp. As he did so, he accelerated the boat, and we had to speak louder to be heard over the roar of the engine. He explained that it was named "casino," part of a larger camp named "Undercliff," started well over one hundred years earlier as a retreat for the corporate executives of the New York Central Railroad. While owned by the railroad, some twelve structures were constructed on the property, including a dining hall, boathouse, and infirmary. In 1932, it was acquired by a group of New Jersey high school music teachers who began to use the property as a children's summer music camp. The first year the music camp opened, Gruen was employed as its crafts counselor. Although he only worked as a counselor for the first two years, since he also resided in New Jersey, he had stayed in touch with the owners. In the early 1960s, children's summer camp business began to decline, and Gruen learned that Undercliff had been subdivided and was being offered for sale. He jumped at the opportunity and acquired the casino, one of the properties with a waterfront structure. He finished his description as we approached the northerly end of the lake, and he slowed the speed of the boat pointing to the casino.

As we drew nearer, the casino struck me much as had my first impression of the *Columbia*. The structure was immense, directly abutting the shoreline, with numerous impressive architectural features. A dock ran the full width of the building while a covered balcony ran along most of the second story. A large brick chimney protruded from a steep roof, abutted by a decorative square turret with attractive windows. But just like the *Columbia*, I saw that the structure was in very poor condition.

We offloaded our gear, and Gruen gave us a tour of the building. The ground floor was mostly used for storage and a workshop. The space was crammed full of all sorts of used material. There were a few old lamps but mostly used pipe, sinks, toilets, and other similar paraphernalia. Peter whispered in my ear, "Now you know what his place in New Jersey looks like."

Once on the second floor, it quickly became apparent why it was called the Casino. The large main room had an immense wheel of fortune hung on one of the walls and numerus game tables. From there we were taken up a winding set of stairs into the turret, which consisted of a large room with a beautiful view of the lake. In the center of the room was a pool table with elaborately carved legs. Over the table hung an oval-stained glass lamp. Obviously the building had been used for entertainment purposes.

Returning to the second floor, we were guided through two more large rooms, both of which shared back-to-back fireplaces. The first of those rooms had access to the covered balcony with bay windows with seats. The second room had an even larger bay window in which was an octagon-shaped table. On the far end of the room was a wall with two small windows, each covered with brass bars. Over the windows were brass plaques engraved with "United States Post Office." I walked up to one of the window and peered through. On the other side I saw a bed, dresser, and nightstand. Gruen, standing alongside me, said, "That's where I sleep."

He then took us to a small room at the rear of the building he had converted to a kitchen, where he offered us a late lunch. Peter asked where the soup had progressed and was told it was somewhere between lentil and potato. Peter declined and announced that he would haul his gear up in the turret. I learned that on previous trips he and his wife had slept a mattress on the pool table.

Gruen then escorted me and my wife back to the adjoining large room where he had placed two cots and an antique dresser. Looking about the room, I noticed that along the crown of a very high ceiling hung a galvanized rain gutter. At the far end of that gutter hung a second gutter, which pitched down into the corner of the room where it rested on a large funnel stuck in a hole in the floor. As Gruen invited us to sleep in that room, I pointed to the gutters. With a shrug he responded, "There are some leaks in the roof, but don't worry you'll stay dry."

Peter and our wives spent the rest of the afternoon hanging out on the dock, as Gruen and I continued to poke around the casino. The structure was impressive, the interior as attractive as the exterior, but all in desperate need of maintenance and repair. Both the interior and exterior showed signs of water damage. I told him I would love to help him preserve the building by repairing the roof. When asked if I knew how to do that, I told him of my camp building experience as a teenager. During the course of that discussion I asked whether the ground floor was filled with that paraphernalia when he had acquired the casino. He told me it hadn't been there and that he had acquired it from camp buildings on the far end of the lake. Apparently the state had acquired those properties for addition to the Adirondack Park and had permitted fixture removal before the structures were demolished.

Later that afternoon we all gathered on the balcony for beer, wine, cheese, and crackers. We were all engaged in conversation when Gruen, pointing down the lake, interrupted with a loud, "Here she comes." In the distance we could see the white boat that he had earlier identified as the tour boat *Doris*. As it drew nearer, we began to hear a voice through a loudspeaker. Gruen, who had been seated now, stood and in an increasingly louder tone stated, "I hate that damn boat. It's not just that noise—wait till you see the wake."

"I have been thinking of sinking that thing with a torpedo."

The rest of us sat there quietly as the *Doris* pulled alongside and rather close to the casino. All of a sudden, Gruen sprang to the edge of the balcony, spun about, dropped his pants, and hung his backside over the railing. Almost instantly the voice on the *Doris* ceased as we watched many of the passengers raise cameras.

The weather remained perfect for the balance of the weekend. While our wives spent most of their time sunning on the dock, Peter and I swam, fished from a canoe, and water-skied behind the *Columbia*. Late each afternoon we all returned to the balcony for drinks and cheese and crackers. The *Doris* continued to tour the lake, but as she approached the Casino she would abruptly turn to the east and hug the far shore of Moose Island. Although Gruen didn't say a word, he would grin at us, partially raise himself, and pat his behind.

We left for New Jersey after lunch on Sunday. Gruen ferried us back to the George and Bliss Marina, where he and I stood in the *Columbia* lifting our gear onto the dock. Peter and our wives began to walk to the parking lot as I started to climb from the boat. Placing his hand on my shoulder, he held me back.

"Steve, when can you come back, how about next weekend?"

I responded by telling him that I was not aware that Peter and Debbie were returning.

"I didn't invite them, but sure would like you to come back. You can fish some and help me with the roof—of course you can bring your wife."

I didn't make a commitment, but gave him my phone number and asked that he call me later in the week.

As we started to travel back to New Jersey, I pondered whether and how I should tell Peter and Debbie that I had been invited to return. It troubled me that I should be invited, but not his relatives. However, it didn't take very long, I believe we were approaching

Keene Valley, when Peter said, "So when are you going back?" Peter recounted that Gruen had told him how much he had enjoyed my company.

Later in the week Gruen called me, and I gave him a date when I would return. I told him he would not have to pick me up at George and Bliss as I planned to tow my outboard boat, stored at my dad's camp in North Hudson.

I returned for several weekends during July and early August, and nearly the last two weeks of August when my judicial clerkship ended. I fished some with my boat, but did a considerable amount of work on the casino's roof. In some ways the most enjoyable time was spent shuttling back and forth across the lake, hauling shingles from a lumberyard in the village. At first using the *Columbia* for that purpose seemed inappropriate to me, but it became appealing when Gruen began to let me pilot the craft.

It was during the Labor Day weekend when one morning at breakfast Gruen said, "You know—I would like you to be my neighbor."

"Where?" I asked him. "Here or in New Jersey?"

"Up here. I would like to sell you my other camp."

I told him I had no idea that he had a second camp and questioned where it was. He expressed some surprise that I hadn't noticed it, and said it was directly next door to the casino. I had seen a small structure to the south of the Casino and asked if that was the camp. "No," he told me, "it's directly next door and up a steep incline from the shore."

As Gruen cleared the breakfast table, I took a short walk down the shore and then up a fairly steep grade to a small open meadow. From there the grade increased again and was densely covered with a variety of sapling. Beyond the crown of those trees I could see the roofline of an immense structure, a structure I later learned was fifty feet wide. I began to make my way through the saplings when I stumbled on the first of a series of large stone steps that led up to that structure.

Although the saplings had grown up, around, and very close to the building, I could see enough of it to appreciate extraordinarily attractive architectural features. Although attractive, its condition was poor. The roof consisted of several large gables, one of which projected at a considerable height over a ground-floor bay window. In the center of the roof was an eyebrow window with an attractive mullion arrangement. The entire roof was covered with cedar shakes, and the valleys were filled with moss from which numerous tiny pine trees had grown.

I made my way up some rickety steps to a front porch, where over the front door was a sign that announced "Silver Birch." The door was unlocked and inside I found more attractive features. In the middle of the main room was a large freestanding fieldstone fireplace with two opposite fireboxes. The windows were very attractive, with numerous small panes. On the second floor, the windows were even more attractive, but there I observed numerous signs of roof leaks. Few of the first- or second-floor rooms had finished interior surfaces, leaving the building's framing visible. That framing was the balloon style, with the smallest timber being a four-by-four.

All the rooms were filled with rustic furniture, many with bunk-beds. Surprisingly, the walls in rooms with beds were covered with names, some with brief messages, all from females. Nearly every room without a bed had an upright piano. After exploring the numerous rooms, I returned to the casino where I told Gruen I had seen Silver Birch and asked if that was his other camp.

He told me that it was and recounted the building's history for me. It had been built by the New York Central Railroad as part of the Camp Undercliff retreat for its executives. When acquired as a children's music camp in 1932, it became the dorm for the senior girls; hence all the pianos. Sometime in the early 1960s, during the music camp's last summer of operations, the senior girls left their names and messages on bedroom walls.

He finished by telling me, "You know that camp has nearly the same potential as the casino; you can cut all those trees and have a great view of your waterfront."

I asked him how much he wanted, and amazingly was told 7,500 dollars. I assured him I believed that was a very reasonable price, but that I was just beginning my professional career and had no cash at all. He paused for a moment and then said, "Okay, I'll just take a mortgage."

And so it was, just like my dad, I bought a camp well before I bought a family home—and luckily all it took was the stroke of a Bic.

Living with Mother Nature

More than any other life experience, camp ownership has taught me much about the vicissitude of nature. The forces of nature are constant yet often unpredictable. Mother Nature is forever taking back my little piece of the Adirondacks. The notion that here in paradise I am only a temporary custodian is slowly taking hold.

I once thought that my experiences in this regard were due to the isolated location of our camp, Silver Birch—it is only accessible by water. As we only have use of the camp from ice-out until the end of October, I have less time to engage in preventative measures, and the ravages wrought by winter weather are more apparent on our return in spring. However, based on conversations with other camp owners and caretakers, I have concluded otherwise.

At my other home, that centrally heated and air-conditioned center hall colonial in suburban New Jersey, mankind has successfully beaten back Mother Nature. Woodlands have been cleared, streams culverted, storm sewers quickly divert excess rainwater, Terminix Corporation rids our homes of critters large and small, while Lawn Doctor makes certain that no insect, grub, or centipede enters our yards. To the extent possible, Mother Nature has been neutralized.

Camp life on the other hand is very different. From the days of Verplanck Colvin, it has been the goal of camp life to experience nature up close. As in the days when camps were simple lean-tos or tents on platforms, any present day camp worthy of the name is well integrated into its surroundings. Sure, Adirondack winters are the most severe found in any of the lower forty-eight states. However, we have intentionally placed our Adirondack retreats in unprotected locations where they are readily accessible to every wood-munching porcupine, den-seeking raccoon, mouse, insect, fungus, and mold spore. If you don't believe me, next time you first open camp, step inside and take a deep breath—you'll know you are not alone.

And so it is that I am forever conscious of my efforts to keep a toehold in the woods. Aside from the repair of winter damage, there is the routine replacement of rotted shingles, painting, preserving of decks, and stairs not to mention the eviction of four-footed critters. Please do not mistake these observations as complaints. I have come to accept, if not actually enjoy, these chores as a part of the Adirondack experience.

One such chore requires me to place circulating pumps in the lake under our docks and boathouse. Those devices bring warmer water from the bottom of the lake to the surface to prevent the formation of ice and the damage it can cause. I typically position those pumps in late October and then walk in during the week between Christmas and New Year's to turn them on. I have come to enjoy this "turning on" tradition, as the walk through the woods, often on snowshoes, gives me a different perspective on our corner of the Adirondacks. As I have grown older my family has become ever more concerned that I take these three-hour round-trip walks in the snow alone. But I enjoy the solitude and find the exercise invigorating and safe, although not always without incident. There was the time that I carried a new pump in rather deep snow and…but I digress and will save the telling of that adventure for another time.

My attempts at keeping Mother Nature at bay with circulating pumps must seem comical to her. Although the prevention of ice formation can eliminate some types of damage, the real risk comes in spring, cannot be prevented and is wholly dependent on the direction of the wind—Mother Nature's whim. The ice melts first at the edges of the lake. As it continues to degrade, large sheets of ice, some four feet thick and many acres in size, are left floating about. Should a brisk wind begin to push such a frozen mass in the direction of my boathouse, substantial damage is certain. To date, either because of the protected location of my boathouse or because Mother Nature has taken pity on me, I have been spared serious damage.

And so it was that, until recently, Mother Nature had reclaimed my camp only at the molecular level. That all changed one recent August afternoon. Mary and I had been working around our guest cottage, actually a second camp that we had acquired adjacent to Silver Birch. I had been applying waterproofing to the decks. Although the weather was expected to be fairly good, as the afternoon wore on, it became apparent that rain would shortly arrive. I rolled out the last of the waterproofing, cleaned up, and decided to take a little nap before the evening meal. I stretched out on a bed in the guest cottage and listened as a rain shower slowly began to beat on the roof. The intensity of the rain began to build, the sound of which I have often succumbed to sleep. However, on this occasion, I lay there contemplating the effect the rain would have on my freshly treated decks.

My thoughts were interrupted by a deafening lightning strike. Broken glass showered all over me, the lights went out, and as I sprang from the bed I was acutely aware of an acrid smell. As I ran from the bedroom I heard Mary screaming at the far end of the cottage. I found her and quickly determined that, although shaken, she was unharmed. We both made our way to a screened porch, which gave us a protected view of the out-of-doors. There in the downpour was a huge mass of smoldering tree branches. Standing amid the debris was the remnant of a giant white pine that had stood less than twenty feet from the window in the bedroom I had been occupying. From our vantage point, we could see large limbs protruding from the eves of the cottage.

My son Chris and a friend were staying at Silver Birch and quickly found us on the porch. Chris said that he smelled smoke. I suggested that it came from the pile of smoldering branches. Mary feared it might be coming from the cottage. We grabbed flashlights and searched about, found no source of smoke, but by now were all aware of an ever-intensifying aroma of wood smoke. Chris observed that there might be fire in the attic space beneath the roof. Chris and I crawled through a trapdoor into the attic. As we searched for the source of smoke, it dawned on me that without electric power our water pump would not function, and there was little hope of fighting a fire. It then became clear to me that Mother Nature could take giant steps in reclaiming my piece of the park.

Mother Nature took pity on us that day. None of the buildings were badly damaged, and the rain continued long enough to extinguish the fire smoldering in the debris pile. When the rain abated, we saw the effects of Mother Nature's warning shot. Pieces of branches were floating in the lake some two hundred feet from the base of the tree, branches lay all about the roof of the cottage, and one had been driven through the roof of our gazebo. All the large fuses in the main electric service had been blown and telephone wires were burnt to a crisp. Our creature comforts were restored in several days, but cleaning up took much longer.

Chris and I worked many days cutting up the larger sections of the tree with chain saws and chipping the smaller branches. As we slowly reduced the pile of rubble, we contemplated the fate of what remained of the trunk. It had been a massive tree, slightly more than ten feet in circumference. Some twenty feet now stood branchless and splintered in a large open area, which the tree's large crown had formerly dominated to the exclusion of all other trees.

Chris suggested that we cut the trunk at waist height and hollow out the stump for use as a flower planter. I agreed, but as he approached the trunk, the Stihl growling, I had a change of heart. This tree was too majestic to become a flowerpot for geraniums and petunias. I would have to find a way to make lemonade from this lemon. It took a few weeks, but slowly I formulated a plan that would make appropriate use of my crippled giant.

The upper reaches of the trunk were badly splintered, and there were signs that the lightning strike may have split the trunk down to the roots. Nevertheless, the bottom ten feet seemed to be reasonably intact. And so I decided that the trunk would become a sculpture—not any old sculpture. I would commission a chain saw carver to carve me a bear—but not any old bear. My bear would be gazing up at the sky, with one paw reaching high above its head. In its paw I would fasten a large jagged lightning bolt I would fashion from heavy aluminum stock.

Finding a chain saw carver willing to come to my camp proved more difficult than I had imagined. October arrived, I was closing camp, and still had not succeeded in locating my artist. (My search wasn't just for a chain saw carver, for now I featured myself a patron of the arts.) Throughout that winter, I searched the internet and the classified pages of *Adirondack Life* and the *Lake Placid News* for my artist. I had no luck and began to believe that perhaps it was for-tuitous that my search fail. After all, was it really smart to jest with Mother Nature in this way? The winds during ice-out might change.

The following summer, while driving to camp, my luck changed. On the Northway, just above Albany, I encountered a strange vehicle traveling very slowly in the right lane. It was a battered early 1960s pickup loaded with little cartoon-style bears. A sign hung on the bumper, which read, "Pull me over—my bears are for sale." This wasn't the setting I had pictured for the commissioning of my work of art, but as all other attempts had failed, I motioned the driver to pull over.

The driver was also a 1960s model—sporting a beard and long ponytail. For several minutes we stood by the roadside trying to talk over the noise of the traffic. I asked him if he had carved the bears on his truck. He responded that he had. I asked if he could carve a life-size bear, which was more lifelike than his passengers. He then motioned me to the cab were he produced a portfolio of photographs of the most intricate carvings of bears, wolves, eagles, and other wildlife. I asked if he would come to Lake Placid and carve a bear from a tree trunk. He responded, "What's the story?" I shrugged, indicating that I failed to understand his question. He then explained that he does not undertake time-consuming projects, such as mine, unless the carving depicts an event or has some significance beyond the object itself. I then told him of the lightning strike and the pose I planned for my bear. As I explained, his eyes brightened, and before I could finish he promised to be at my camp the following weekend. We agreed upon a price, exchanged phone numbers, and parted. Although this hippie did not fit my image of an artist, his requirement that the work have significance allowed me to indulge my image as a patron of the arts and justify the cost.

During the week I telephoned my artist and arranged for his boat ride to our camp. He planned to arrive early Friday morning, while I planned to arrive around midday on Saturday. As a result I arranged for Chris, who lives in Lake Placid, to pick him up at our dock in town.

Chris picked me up at the dock on Saturday. I inquired how the carving was progressing. He opined that I would be pleased and related that neighbors were stopping by to witness the event. He also advised me that he had built a platform from which the artist could safely reach most of the usable portions of the trunk.

As we pulled into the boathouse, I could hear the sound of a chain saw. I rushed up the grade to where the tree had stood. My artist was standing, bare-chested high on the platform Chris had constructed, a cigarette hanging from the corner of his mouth. He nodded to me as he continued to cut small chunks from what appeared to be the outline of a life-size bear. Strewn about were scores of empty Budweiser cans, and sitting on the platform was a half-empty bottle of tequila. "What's with the booze?" I asked Chris.

"He drinks tequila with beer chasers while he works" was the response. When I frowned, Chris responded, "Oh, he's good—he has all of his fingers." Once again, my patron of the arts image began to wane.

As the day wore on, the outline of a bear became more defined and by evening was just what I had envisioned. My bear was peering straight up into the sky with its right paw held up high, almost as though a salute. The outstretched paw was given a flat surface just beneath curved claws—the perfect spot to fasten a lightning bolt. The bear had erect ears and finely carved eyes, mouth, and nostrils. Each paw had well-defined claws, and the entire surface had been striated to give the appearance of fur. The end product was so well done that my visions of the patron began to return—so much so that I paid the artist five hundred dollars more than had been agreed upon. How would I ever tell Mary?

As the artist began to collect his tools, Chris dismantled the platform, and I began to rake up the chips and debris left by the carving. As I did so, I became aware of an unfamiliar sound. It was a modestly loud throbbing noise, a series of short bursts—the sound a rusty hinge might make. When I raked the noise would stop, but when I stopped the sound would soon return. I couldn't quite place the source. I stopped raking and asked, "Do you hear that sound?" Both Chris and the artist approached. Leaning toward the bear and tapping the base of the trunk with his steel-tipped boot, the artist replied, "Oh, them's wood borers—they're in there eat'n wood."

Mother Nature's insect attack on my work of art, quickly brought me to the realization that I ought not irritate her by pointing a phony lightning bolt toward the sky. Such jesting might promote her to send a spring ice flow toward my boathouse. I therefore left the bear to simply wave to her; for as long as she might let it stand.

Last Hike

About five years after Mom passed away, Dad got remarried. After marrying Martha he didn't hike much anymore; her daily schedule didn't permit it. Never have I witnessed a person whose life was so regimented. There was no written schedule, but each minute of the day was devoted to some activity or chore, conceived of by Martha and which no one dared alter. Each meal was served at a given time, and woe and behold those who might arrive late. While Dad and Martha were at his camp in North Hudson, I could avoid the schedule by popping in for an hour or so. But in so doing upset the schedule, causing Martha to say, "You should have phoned us first, so that I could make plans." However, winter visits to her condo in Florida were another matter. Whether we stayed in the condo or a nearby hotel, Martha would manage to draw us into her daily routine. I recall one occasion while on a business trip to

Florida I stayed an extra day or two with Dad and Martha. As we concluded lunch on one of those days, Martha announced that Dad and I would go swimming while she grocery shopped. "I will drop you off at the beach, but be ready to be picked up at four thirty," she commanded. "We can't miss the early-bird special."

In Palm Beach the change in water depth is very gradual. One has to wade out a great distance to reach a depth where standing is no longer possible. On that day the water was very warm, and we waded out to a point where we could stand between gentle swells. There we bobbed up and down engaged in reminiscence and storytelling. Time flew, and as four thirty approached, Dad was facing seaward and I was facing the beach. I hadn't planned it that way, but suddenly I noticed that Martha was standing where we had left our towels. My first inclination was to interrupt Dad's story—I had heard this one many times before, but then some devilish impulse took control of me. I said nothing. Soon I observed Martha cupping her hands around her mouth in an obvious attempt to gain our attention. But over the sound of breaking waves and squawking seabirds, nothing could be heard. Next she began to frantically wave one of our towels over her head. This she did while wading knee-deep into the surf. That attempt having failed, I observed as she roamed the beach speaking with sunbathers. With each encounter I observed as she pointed in our direction. Obviously Martha was attempting to enlist an emissary to bring us ashore. Finally after four or five attempts, a recruit was found. A muscular twentysomething swam to us and declared that some "crazy lady" wanted us on the beach.

And so it was that with the marriage to Martha, Dad's hiking days had come to an end. Unlike Mom, Martha could never tolerate the vagaries associated with the traversing of Adirondack peaks on foot. While Dad never expressed the thought, I thought of him as deprived.

It had been a while, and I am no longer sure of the reason, but an occasion arose when Dad was alone at his camp, as was I. Most likely Martha was on one of her sojourns to family in Germany. I seized the opportunity and invited Dad to our camp and a hike up Whiteface. I was to meet him early at the old George and Bliss, at that time Holiday Harbor. We had planned to boat over to Whiteface Landing, hike to the summit, and return to our camp for the night. No schedule—like the old days, just a hike.

It was a day in late September. The foliage was turning color, but that morning it was grayer and cooler than I had hoped for. Dad was waiting at the gas dock when I arrived. We put his duffel under the forward deck, and as we had done many years ago with his coworkers, headed up the lake to Whiteface Landing. As I may have told you in an earlier tale, Whiteface Landing is a dock on Lake Placid, maintained by the Department of Environmental Conservation at a remote trailhead to Whiteface Mountain.

The first stretch of trail is quite level, leading to a brook and lean-to. As was his custom, Dad insisted on carrying the day pack with bottled water and sandwiches I had prepared. Where the trail permitted, we walked abreast talking about his grandchildren. Beyond the lean-to the trail begins an ever-increasing pitch. At first the grade is moderate, but before long the trail becomes quite steep. When last we hiked together, Dad had set the pace. His ability to set a blistering pace always impressed me, even when I was a young adult. But he always modulated his pace to accommodate companions with less energy. He was forever introducing friends and acquaintances to hiking in the Adirondacks, and did so in a way that encouraged even those with little enthusiasm for the outdoors. On that day his pace was off.

As the trail reached its steepest point, Dad began to take frequent rest stops. I offered to carry the day pack, which he uncharacteristically surrendered. At times I would take a position behind him and observed that when stepping up on a rock or exposed root, he would press down upon his bent knee with his hand to assist in rising over the obstacle. While he made no mention of fatigue, I knew that he was struggling.

Had my hiking companion been anyone else, I might have suggested that we call it a day. But Dad never let others stop short of the summit. He had ways to cajole even overweight companions to summits over four thousand feet. When asked, "How far is it?" he would frequently reply, "It's just a piece up the trail." With such words and constant banter Dad would coax reluctant hikers, step by step, to summits were the view made it all worthwhile. I simply couldn't ask him to quit.

Well toward the summit we approached a rock ledge, a point where on clear days one can see all of Lake Placid below, some of the High Peaks to the south and the summit above. On that day only a small portion of the northerly end of the lake was visible, and the summit was only intermittently visible as clouds blew by. "Doesn't look like we'll get much of a view," I commented, hoping he might give me an opportunity to suggest that we turn around. "Never can tell," he replied. "You know how changeable the weather can be in these mountains." His tone and look indicated that he saw through my comment. He spared me his old saw about waiting five minutes if you didn't like the weather in the Adirondacks, but we both knew that this cloud cover was here for a while. But in this fashion he was telegraphing to me that he was going to the top.

A cold wind was pushing the clouds over the summit as we reached the weather observatory at the top. Nothing was visible and the air, seemingly filled with tiny droplets, left a wet film on our windbreakers. The lack of visibility kept tourists who normally drive up the mountain away. Alone we crouched in the lee of a rock ledge where we quickly ate our sandwiches.

We made our way down with little conversation. Once we got back into the tree cover, it began to rain and Dad made frequent stops to message his right calf. After several such stops he admitted that he was experiencing cramps. These episodes of charley horse did not abate, and from his grimace it was obvious that Dad was in some pain. Once in the boat Dad was doubled over, kneading his calf and foot, which visibly twitched in rhythmic spasms. "I'll be fine once I warm up," he assured me.

The distance from White Face Landing to my camp is short. I tied the boat to the dock, gave Dad a handout of the boat, and retrieved his duffel from under the deck. I slowly carried that duffel up the hill to the camp while Dad limped behind me.

Once inside the camp, I went to the kitchen, where during the previous evening I had prepared a pot of beef stew—a favorite of

Dad's. I took the pot from the refrigerator and began to heat it on the stove. A counter on the wall between the kitchen and living room had a cutout, through which I observed Dad sitting in a chair in front of the fireplace.

The stew had just begun to simmer when from the corner of my eye I noticed that Dad had gotten up and down on one knee was leaning into the fireplace. Poking my head through the cutout, I inquired what he was doing.

"I'm going to make a fire. You've got lots of wood and kindling stacked up here—keep cooking." I returned to the stove, but frequently looked over my shoulder to see how he was progressing.

He continued to kneel on one knee while poking about in the firebox with one of the fireplace tools. All of a sudden I saw him drop to both knees and reach deep into the fireplace. He then slowly backed out of the fireplace and stood up holding a large odd-shaped object. I turned off the burner and walked into the living room.

Dad was standing there holding a broken piece of a piano harp with tuning pins and shards of wire. As he turned his face from the object he held to me, his expression changed from one of curiosity to anger.

"You burned a piano!"

I was about to explain to him that I had opened camp one day that spring and had no firewood at the time. That day and evening were quite cold, and I had decided to burn a piano that had been exposed to the weather for years on the back porch.

"Your mom and I bought you many years of piano lessons and gave you several pianos—have you lost your respect for this instrument?"

As he spoke, I slowly pointed to the upright piano that stood a short distance to the right of the fireplace.

Shaking the broken piece of harp, he said, "So what? You could have given this one to some poor kid in town whose parents couldn't afford one. Please finish cooking while I start the fire."

I returned to the kitchen, somewhat shocked as I only witnessed one other occasion when Dad had so angrily expressed himself. It was an occasion when I was in the second grade. We were living in an apartment complex where the superintendent appeared one evening to complain that I had brought home a black schoolmate. I well remember how he escorted the super out of the apartment with a similar tone of voice and facial expression.

I continued heating the stew, warmed two bowls under hot water, and began assembling utensils and drinks on a tray. At first I thought we would eat in the kitchen, but since Dad had started a fire I thought it best to eat while sitting there.

When I returned to the living room with the tray, Dad's fire had taken hold, and the flames were crackling and sparks flying up the flue. Dad was seated in an armchair close to the fireplace. I pushed a coffee table next to him with my foot, on which I placed the tray, and pulled up an armchair for myself. Without speaking we each took a bowl of stew from the tray and began eating.

As we silently ate I would occasionally turn and look at Dad. His gaze seemed focused either in his bowl of stew or in the flames, his face expressionless. When he finished eating he placed his bowl back on the tray and, looking me in the eyes, said, "That was great, can I have another?" As he did so, a warm smile came to his face.

I returned with a second serving for each of us, and between swallows he told me how it wasn't easy to get old, and that he hoped I wouldn't be offended by his reactions. He never mentioned the word *piano* again, as he began recollecting some of the backpacking trips our family had taken in the High Peaks. We spent the rest of the evening sharing recollections of our Adirondack experiences. As the evening wore on, I pushed my two sofas toward the fireplace and rolled out two sleeping bags. As we slipped into the sleeping bags, Dad continued with his remembrance of his early trips to the Adirondacks. We both slept well.

One Dark and Starless Night

As some of you may know, our camp on Lake Placid is accessible only by water. The limited accesses is both an asset and somewhat of an inconvenience. I have always considered the negative aspects minor inconveniences, compared with the romantic image of owning a camp on the extreme end of a lake in one of the most scenic locations in my part of the world. The boat ride I take each Friday evening, from ice-out to mid-October is the high point of my weekly trek and is so invigorating that once at camp sleep is impossible. On starry or moon-filled nights the trip can be intoxicating. On dark or foggy nights, a successful crossing ignites otherwise suppressed feelings of machismo. Such feelings are only enhanced when Mary worries aloud that we are lost and will never make it to camp. I always assured her and reminded her that since 1967 I made such crossings hundreds of times. "Relax," I tell her.

To my way of thinking, the "inconveniences" associated with our remote location are merely logistical. *Real* camps are all in remote locations; our camp was in the best of locations. The buggy lugging of groceries in and garbage out never bothered me. Hauling in construction materials to renovate the camp and build our boathouse simply fueled my notion of being a pioneering do-it-yourselfer. Best of all there are no surprise visits from Aunt Tilley from Toledo.

One such crossing took place in early May of my sixty-fourth year. By that time, I must have made the trip from the village through Sunset Strait, past the westerly shores of Buck and Moose Islands, a thousand times. On this occasion I had arrived by myself earlier in the day to open camp. As the sun set, I had completed the reconnection of plumbing fittings drained the previous October, turned on the water pump, and checked for leaks. As I did not bring provisions with me, I called my son Chris to see if he would join me for dinner in town. We agreed to meet at Nicolas; he would bring our friend John Viscome.

At that time, we had two boats. One was a covered inboard outboard, the other a smaller sixteen-foot open aluminum boat powered by a seventy-five horsepower outboard motor with a control console midship on the starboard side. As usual, that day the open boat was the first to be put into the water. Without a windshield or cover, the ride was uncomfortable in inclement weather. However, with one replacement of the outboard, the vessel had served us well for many years as a work and fishing boat, and on that day the weather was fine.

The sun had just disappeared behind Mackenzie Mountain as I turned on the boathouse exterior lights and began the trip to town. Not only was the weather good, it was somewhat mild for that time of year. The sun's last rays illuminated the clouds with a variety of red and orange tones. Although visibility was good, I had fitted the 365-degree mast light in its socket and turned on the running lights. A nylon bag with flashlight and rain gear had been stowed under the steering console. As I made my way to town, I noted that the Department of Environmental Conservation had yet to drop the lighted buoys in the water, which marked the channels and hazardous obstacles in the lake.

As usual, dinner with Chris and John was enjoyable. There was much talk of camp improvement projects, fishing, and of course, a bit of local gossip. After an hour and a half, we left Nicola's to discover a light drizzle. I wasn't surprised, for as Dad used to say about Adirondack weather, "If you don't like it, wait five minutes." I bid farewell to Chris and John and made my way to Price Choppers where I purchased provisions for the next day's breakfast and lunch.

Although the drizzle had abated, I nevertheless suited up with the stowed rain gear, which included yellow bibbed overalls and a hooded slicker. As I left Paradox Bay, I was faced with my first challenge of the evening. The shallow channel, flanked by rocky shoals leading to the main body of the lake, is usually marked by lighted buoys. This early in the season the only markings were small fluorescent buoys. I navigated the channel with the use of a flashlight. The beam illuminated the fluorescent markers, and shortly I was moving at a brisk pace in open water.

The course that I usually followed to camp took me from the East Lake via Sunset Strait to the West Lake. Once on the West Lake it was a relatively straight shot to the camp. The only obstacle was a corner of Moose Island at Shelter Strait. A lighted buoy usually marked that corner. Although those buoys had yet to be set in their usual locations, there were enough light sources from camps and boathouses on shore to permit me to maintain my bearings. I was feeling very comfortable; after all I had made this crossing hundreds of times, perhaps thousands, some in blinding rain or fog. I didn't need lighted buoys. The only missing element was Mary's plaintive words.

I stayed well in the center of the East Lake until I was able to see the lights of Whiteface Inn on the far shore of the West Lake. At that point I hung a left and passed through the Sunset Strait into the West Lake. I continued toward Whiteface Inn until I was able to look up the West Lake and see the lights of my boathouse. I continued a bit further on that course before turning toward the boathouse to be certain to avoid the point of Moose Island. There are a few camps on that shore of Moose, but on this evening all was dark. Although this course seemed prudent at the time, it took me much closer to the mainland shore than I was accustomed to. As I made a right turn and headed toward my boathouse lights, I was feeling very confident. I recognized the lights of a number of camps on the mainland, even though I could not make out the shores of Buck Island on my right or Moose up ahead.

As I approached Shelter Strait, I began to notice a strange occurrence—the lights on my boathouse went out. Even as I puzzled over this happening I noticed that more and more lights on the mainland were extinguishing. For a moment I thought that I was witnessing the effects of a power outage, but then in a moment I found myself in an unusually thick fog. I turned to look back down the West Lake, only to see all the lights behind me obliterated. Apparently, a fog bank had slid down the Mackenzie range and filled the lake bed.

I slowed the speed of the boat to what I then guestimated to be ten mph. Now believing that I had positioned myself too close to the mainland, I changed course to what I thought would bring myself more toward the center of the Lake. I continued at my much-reduced speed and attempted to use my flashlight. However, the fog was so thick that the light did nothing but create a blinding halo of light.

I don't think I was knocked unconscious, but at some point my senses were such that I came to the realization that had I hit land. I was still seated behind the wheel, and ahead of me the navigation lights shone through cedar branches; I heard the outboard still running. As I reached for the flashlight, I was not conscious of pain.

I found the flashlight between my feet and turned it on. As I did, my heart stopped. The steering console, my rain gear, the floor, everything was covered in blood. I dropped the light and began to pat myself down in an attempt to assess my condition. My limbs and torso seemed to be intact, but as I reached for my face I realized I was in deep trouble. A large portion of the right side of my face, including a large portion of my nose and cheek, were hanging loose from my face. I retrieved the light and attempted to hold my face together with the free hand. As I did so I became aware of the continued heavy flow of blood and the fact that I was seeing double. Common lore has it that your life passes instantly before your eyes as you are about to drown. Whether the surrounding water wasn't deep enough to trigger that response, or the color red brings on another, I responded in a way unusual for me. Like my father, I am not prone to gratuitous profanity, but as my heart now began a thunderous beat, I let loose with a Tourette-like stream of profanity.

The outburst over, I slowly regained my composure and began assessing my situation. I quickly decided that I had to stay put. I felt fairly certain I had hit Moose Island. I was in no condition to stumble about that sparsely populated island looking for camps, which at that time of year were surely still closed. From what I could see of the boat, it was damaged and probably sustained a breach below the waterline. My best bet was a cell phone. However, beyond Sunset Strait I had never found cell phone service on the lake, and rarely carried one. Chris once claimed to get a signal while standing on the roof of our camp. Such acrobatics and the desire to be left alone convinced me to rely on a hard-line connection. But on this evening I had done something I never did before; I had popped my cell phone from its cradle in the car and clipped it to my belt.

Getting to the phone from under all the rain gear was frustrating. Once in my hand, the phone had to be turned on, which included entering a security code. Double vision, the pounding of my heart, and dripping blood made the chore very difficult. Whether my cell carrier had made improvements in its systems or fog provides a better medium for transmission, on that night the screen on my cell showed a respectable signal. I shut off the engine and pressed and held the 9 key. In a moment I heard the voice of a 911 operator who requested my location. It quickly became apparent that the operator knew little about Lake Placid, much less about the West Lake and Moose Island. He kept asking me where I was relative to vehicular access. Becoming frustrated by the conversation, I decided to try another approach. Knowing that the Lake Placid Fire Department maintained a fireboat on the lake, I asked that my situation be relayed to them, and I hung up. I knew that John had a cell phone and had his number on my speed dial. Wiping more blood from the screen, I was able to scroll around and find the number. John's phone immediately kicked into answering service mode. I left him a very detailed message.

Again I pressed and held the 9 key. I reached the same operator who advised me that he had reached the fire department and that the fire boat would shortly be under way. I was told to say on the line as the operator would serve as a communications link between me and the fireboat. The operator tried to engage me in conversation so as to determine my condition. As we spoke I continued to hold my face together with my free hand.

It seemed like an eternity, but I finally heard the distant sound of an inboard boat I hoped would be my rescue. The operator quickly confirmed that the fire boat had entered the West Lake. Based on the approaching sound, I offered a few course corrections and began to shine my flashlight into the fog in the direction of the approaching sound. In a few minutes the bow of the fire boat emerged and was slowly brought within my reach. Releasing the grip on my cheek and nose, I stepped up on my outboard motor and with both hands grabbed the bow rail of the fire boat. At that moment, several pairs of hands grabbed me, and I was quickly strapped to a board, a board to which I would remain strapped, papoose-like, for the next twelve hours.

The boat and ambulance ride to Adirondack Medical Center in Saranac Lake were quick, during which I was aware that some first aid was being performed on my wounds. Throughout the trip I opted to keep my eyes closed. As I was being removed from the ambulance, I heard Chris's voice offering me some assuring words. John had received my message and relayed my mishap to Chris. At that moment I tried to open my eyes and discovered that my face had become so swollen that sight was impossible.

I was wheeled into the emergency room where, after a brief examination and scan, the attending physician advised me that there was nothing that could be done for me in Saranac Lake. In fact she advised me I might lose my nose if I wasn't transferred to a major medical center. It took a moment as I began to assess my fate. Very quickly I recalled the 1965 western movie *Cat Ballou*, where Lee Marvin had his nose bitten off in a bar fight. In that flick the missing appendage was replaced with a tin prosthesis. Although I never considered myself vain, that image sent a shiver through me.

At this point, the attending physician placed a call on an open line to the trauma center at the medical center in Burlington, Vermont. The exchange I overheard gave me greater insight into my condition. I was described as having a very severe laceration, which among other things exposed my sinuses. In addition there was a likelihood of broken facial bones, but the scans had not been thoroughly read. Saranac wanted to medevac me to Burlington via New York State Forest Ranger helicopter. Burlington inquired whether the helicopter was pressurized. When told it wasn't, the idea was scrapped as a change in pressure might cause additional complications. The decision was made to transport me by private ambulance.

It took some time for the ambulance to arrive. During this time, Chris stayed by my side, offering assuring words. At one point I became aware of another voice. As that person came closer, he introduced himself as a New York State Trooper. He inquired whether I had been drinking that evening. I told him that I had some wine with dinner, but no more than two glasses. He asked whether I would consent to a breathalyzer test. I told him that I would consent, and he placed a tube between my lips. At his command I blew on the tube. Moments later, with a disappointed tone of voice, the officer announced that I was sober. I was torn between feelings of relief and indignation, but then I was told the ambulance had arrived.

The ambulance was staffed with a driver and an attendant. At first they insisted that Chris couldn't accompany me in the ambulance. However, after some cajoling by Chris, they relented and he joined me on the trip.

There are several routes one might take from Saranac to Burlington, all of which require a crossing of Lake Champlain. As we left the Adirondack Medical Center, the driver and his assistant debated which route they would take. Both agreed that the route that incorporated the Essex ferry was the quickest. However, it was very late and neither knew when the last ferry had left for Vermont. They placed a cell phone call and were advised that the last ferry was full and would shortly be leaving. Mustering a serious tone, the driver stated that a seriously injured patient was en route and that the ferry should be held with sufficient space to carry the ambulance. Assured of the requested accommodation, we headed for the Essex ferry.

I had no sense of the passage of time, but it was well into the next day when I finally arrived at the trauma center in Burlington. Still strapped to the same board, I was given numerous scans. I am a fairly thin person, and the confinement to that board was now causing me great discomfort. Every bone and joint was pressed into the board, and the inability to move was maddening. However, more troubling was the lack of attention my nose was getting. Although the saline dressing was refreshed on arrival, nothing more was being done to save me from a tin prosthesis. As I was being wheeled into yet another scan, I asked when someone would begin to take action to save my nose.

The reaction was discomforting; a snicker left me convinced that my next trip on the gurney was to a surgery, were my now atrophied appendage would be excised. I summoned all of my courage and queried why I should part so easily with my nose. As I was still unable to open my eyes, I am not certain who it was that responded: "You won't lose your nose, there is too much blood supplied to that area for that to occur." I reflected on that advice, and remembering the sea of crimson in the boat, tried to suppress thoughts of a tin nose.

After several additional scans, I was wheeled into a room where I was joined by Chris. He advised me that my wound would now be closed. We were joined by a doctor with a very youthful voice. Chris later opined that he could not have been thirty. The procedure took forever. My face had been opened from the center of my nose, up and across the right cheek, well beyond the far corner of the right eye. He began to stitch my nose from inside and then on the exterior of the nose and cheek. From the conversation he was having with Chris, I concluded that he was a young resident in the trauma center.

Chris had called Mary while I was still in Saranac. Mary and daughter Anne arrived in Burlington shortly after my wound was closed: it was then near nine in the morning. With my wife and children assembled; several physicians delivered their findings. My nose would be spared, but some five bones in my face had been broken. Four of those breaks would heal without intervention, but the floor of my left eye orbit had been "blown out" and was protruding into the sinus. It was this break that had caused my double vision. I could remain in Burlington or return home for remedial eye-socket surgery.

Now released from the board, I was assured that I could get up and move about. A catheter was removed, and for the first time I tried to open my eyes. With help from Mary, I got up and went to the bathroom. The image that appeared in the bathroom mirror was horrifying. My face was terribly swollen, discolored, and traversed by a series of stiches that looked like railroad tracks. Worst of all, depending upon where I cast my gaze, I still had double vision.

After a brief conversation, all agreed that I should return to New Jersey. We returned via the Grand Isle ferry and stayed the night at Chris's house in Keene. The following day Mary, Anne, and I made our way to New Jersey.

I had two concerns. First and foremost I needed to have my eye orbit repaired. Of secondary concern was the scar across my nose and face. As it turned out, the scar required no further attention. Every plastic surgeon consulted commented on the excellence of the sutures. As it healed, the scar became less and less noticeable, particularly as I wear glasses. I was indeed fortunate to land in the care of that resident surgeon in Burlington.

I interviewed several surgeons reputed to have performed orbit repairs. Several, upon viewing the Burlington films, declined the assignment. I declined the services of others who performed the procedure only occasionally. I finally settled on a young surgeon at the New Jersey College on Medicine and Dentistry in Newark. He encountered my condition several times a week as he repaired the victims of street fights and drug deals gone bad. A few hours in an outpatient surgery center cured my double vision. A thin piece of porous plastic was slipped under my eye ball and glued in place with dental adhesive over the hole in the floor of my socket. Over time the bone would grow over and through the plastic. My vision was fully restored.

Although well recovered from my misadventure, I have not regained my nocturnal navigation bravado—Mary won't let me. Now when we travel to camp together, she insists upon leaving so that we arrive well before sunset. In addition she then purchased a handheld GPS navigation device for use when I made the trip alone. The screen showed an outline of the lake, islands and all. The cursor depicted the boat's position as I navigate around the islands to camp. More recently cell phone reception has improved, and my smartphone serves that purpose. To date I have not had the need to use it, but I do keep it within reach. Mary also keeps a photo of my face taken the day following the incident on her smart phone. Anytime I suggest that she "relax," my confidence gets a bruising as she brandishes that photo about.

Postscript

L ike Dad, I purchased our Lake Placid camp long before I purchased our first family home. While I have nothing but warm recollections of life at that North Hudson camp, I much prefer summer life at the far end of Lake Placid. Despite the lack of electric power and running water, Dad selected the North Hudson camp for its view of the High Peaks. When he purchased the camp on that small rise, it had great views of Giant and Dix mountains. However, over time white pines grew at the rear of the camp, obscuring the view of those peaks. Davy and I always wanted closer proximity to water, something I now have plenty of. Moreover, from my dock and boathouse, now I have the best view of Whiteface.

Davy spent some time with us at our camp, and I am certain that he would also have purchased a camp, but unfortunately, he passed away at an early age. However, his love of the Adirondacks was reflected in the choice of the name for his daughter Marcy. His son Brian has engaged in the same choice making, naming his sons Colden and Keene.

I have continued to climb the High Peaks, but nothing like Dad. Instead I spent the majority of my time renovating my camp. At first it was Silver Birch, the camp I acquired from Richard Gruen. I spent several years bringing water and electric service to the structure, and then replacing all the roofing and some of the foundation piers.

Along the way I purchased a 1955 mahogany Chris-Craft Sportsman, which I spent several years restoring and rebuilding the engine. Although that craft really can move, because of the time that it took me to get it in the water, my kids insisted that it be named Slow Poke. That craft has always been one of my most valued possessions, and I will never forget when my early teenage daughter Anne asked if she could take it to cruise the shoreline. I hope my motivation was akin to Mom and Dad's encouragement of early independence, but in any event, I gave Anne the key. Today Anne can navigate the lake at night as well as I can.

Several years later, I managed to acquire Camp Sunrise, a property abutting Silver Birch. That camp structure was smaller, in a similar condition, but on a lot with a much larger shorefront. At that point I stopped working on Silver Birch, renovated Sunrise, and began constructing a boathouse. The boathouse took me several years to construct, with help from my son and wife, Mary. Mary still likes to recollect her boating a dump truck load of crushed stone in burlap bags from town to camp. Those stones were used to fill cribs around the base of concrete filled columns supporting the boathouse.

Although I personally spent a lot time on these projects, I also spent much time introducing my children, Anne and Chris, and my wife's Texan nephews and niece, Peter, Adam and Mary, to the Adirondacks. Due to the summer heat in Houston, those nephews and niece spent their entire summers with us. All those kids spent the summers of their grade and high school years swimming, canoeing, fishing, waterskiing, and mountain climbing in the Adirondacks. To this day they have regularly returned to the camp, now with their children.

Having focused more on the restoration of Camp Sunrise, in recent years I sought to pass Camp Silver Birch to someone who would continue what I had begun and preserve an extraordinary camp structure. After several years I finally found Brian Keating, a man with a long family Adirondack history. Like me he fell in love with Silver Birch, but unlike me he has time left to finish the work. I am now here to help him where and when I can.

Finally, like Dad, I wanted to find some means of livelihood so as to live full-time in the Adirondacks. Although not admitted as an attorney in New York, I constantly sought some practice niche that would encourage me to seek such admission. I never did find a niche and continued to live in New Jersey.

Unlike me, my son Chris moved to Lake Placid at an early age. At first he worked for camp contractors, then formed his own construction company and now owns and operates the most prominent cabinet shop in the North Country. Dad and I may have failed, but Chris has succeeded.

CPSIA information can be obtained
at www.ICGtesting.com
Printed in the USA
LVHW092015161120
671835LV00005B/1234

9 781646 548439